Cambridge Elements ≡

Elements in Leadership
edited by
Ronald E. Riggio
Claremont McKenna College
Susan E. Murphy
University of Edinburgh

Founding Editor
Georgia Sorenson
University of Cambridge

QUESTIONING
LEADERSHIP

A Framework for Growth and Purpose

Michael Harvey
Washington College

CAMBRIDGE
UNIVERSITY PRESS

Shaftesbury Road, Cambridge CB2 8EA, United Kingdom

One Liberty Plaza, 20th Floor, New York, NY 10006, USA

477 Williamstown Road, Port Melbourne, VIC 3207, Australia

314–321, 3rd Floor, Plot 3, Splendor Forum, Jasola District Centre, New Delhi – 110025, India

103 Penang Road, #05–06/07, Visioncrest Commercial, Singapore 238467

Cambridge University Press is part of Cambridge University Press & Assessment, a department of the University of Cambridge.

We share the University's mission to contribute to society through the pursuit of education, learning and research at the highest international levels of excellence.

www.cambridge.org
Information on this title: www.cambridge.org/9781009484251

DOI: 10.1017/9781009484299

First published 2024

A catalogue record for this publication is available from the British Library.

ISBN 978-1-009-48425-1 Hardback
ISBN 978-1-009-48424-4 Paperback
ISSN 2631-7796 (online)
ISSN 2631-7788 (print)

Questioning Leadership

A Framework for Growth and Purpose

Elements in Leadership

DOI: 10.1017/9781009484299
First published online: May 2024

Michael Harvey
Washington College
Author for correspondence: Michael Harvey, mharvey2@washcoll.edu

Abstract: Leaders help groups solve their hardest problems through critical inquiry that sparks creative solutions. The need for leadership increases when a group's situation changes, so that its familiar answers and ways of solving problems begin to fail. In this core sense, leadership is philosophical, and helping navigate the group to effective truths that enable it to survive and thrive is the core of the leader's work.

Keywords: questions, curiosity, critical thinking, phronesis, meaning-making

ISBNs: 9781009484251 (HB), 9781009484244 (PB), 9781009484299 (OC)
ISSNs: 2631-7796 (online), 2631-7788 (print)

Contents

In the last days of the fourth world I wished to make a map
for those who would climb through the hole in the sky.

My only tools were the desires of humans as they emerged
from the killing fields, from the bedrooms and the kitchens.

For the soul is a wanderer with many hands and feet.

The map must be of sand and can't be read by ordinary light.
It must carry fire to the next tribal town, for renewal of spirit.

In the legend are instructions on the language of the land, how it
was we forgot to acknowledge the gift, as if we were not in it or of it.
. . . . . .
We were never perfect.
Yet, the journey we make together is perfect on this earth
who was once a star and made the same mistakes as humans.
We might make them again, she said.
Crucial to finding the way is this: there is no beginning or end.
You must make your own map.

Joy Harjo, "A Map to the Next World"

1 What Needs to Be Done?

Successful leaders don't start out asking, "What do I want to do?" They ask,
"What needs to be done?"

Peter Drucker (2004)

Human beings are born collaborators and intensely social – yet we are also
moody, introspective, and self-regarding. We build strong structures to help
hold groups[1] together – then energetically challenge and undermine these very
structures. Ours is an "unsocial sociability," as the Enlightenment philosopher
Immanuel Kant put it (1991, p. 44). We constantly judge others and monitor
how we perceive they're judging us. We tend to exaggerate our talents (Alicke
and Govorun 2005) and other people's shortcomings (Ross 1977). Two questions bounce around our heads every day: 'What are we trying to get done here?'
and 'What's in it for me?' The groups we form, from companies to countries, are

---

[1] 'Group' as defined in this Element: (1) two or more members, with (2) a shared purpose whose
achievement requires (3) interdependent work, and (4) a duration sufficient for habits and
expectations to form. This is a relatively standard definition in the social sciences, for instance
in industrial/organizational psychology (Riggio 2013, p. 309). 'Group' is a decidedly broad term:
corporations, startups, nonprofits, government agencies, churches, athletic teams, municipal
governments, other types of formal organizations, but also entire nations considered as
a whole, or early human hunter-gatherer-fishers – all of these are groups. People sitting in
a subway car or passenger airplane are not, by this definition, a group, unless something goes
terribly wrong and their situation snaps into a different reality, so that they must work together to
try to survive. Paul Greengrass' 2006 film *United 93* is a riveting dramatization of a tragic
instance (see also Harvey 2011, pp. 210–11).

frail vessels teeming with feelings, desires, self-dealing, and creative mischief – but they are also the most rationally organized and powerful forces in the world. Our highly developed capacities for cognition, creativity, and collaboration have given us an incredible ability to solve old problems in new ways, and identify and solve new problems (Fuentes 2017).

But our very success means that we have unleashed radical change on an unprecedented scale and at a quickening pace: the immense size of our largest groups and our total population, expected to exceed ten billion by century's end; global political and economic instability (most of the world's 200 or so countries are poorly governed: see Hartmann and Thierry 2022); the waning of lives centered in families (some argue that this is a positive change: see Skirbekk 2022); our rising energy demands; our enormously destructive impact on nature (Kolbert 2014); the capacity we have given individuals to inflict devastating violence (Peterson and Densley 2021); and the development of increasingly autonomous machine systems entrusted to interact with and manage our world even as we struggle to understand how they work (De Angelis et al. 2023). Just over the horizon of certainty we glimpse the coming of a nonbiological sentience lacking emotionality and perhaps moral understanding, but exceeding us in cognitive capacity (Suleyman and Bhaskar 2023). The rise of capitalism in the last four or five centuries has rocket-fueled an ideology of radically individual freedom and autonomy, centered in the wealthiest and most technologically advanced societies, and championed by the most successful and fortunate individuals, that defines many of these things as other people's problems. Against the onrushing tide of new ideas and ways of living, traditional understandings have retreated, but still animate billions of people with unease and hostility at the rapid change around them. Amid our ever-increasing material plenty we are increasingly alone, severed from nature, and insecure. Increasingly the young live and connect by simulations and virtual experiences. Old ways of living and knowing fade, and we gaze to the future with more anxiety than hope.

Upon this landscape of uncertainty and vulnerability, leadership presents itself as a magical solution. Part of us wants it to be that simple. The greater our problems, the more we hope for leaders who are strong, compassionate, fair, and above all wise, so that they can teach us the answers to our problems. We yearn for the leader's living example and physical closeness, their eye contact, their smile. Being there with us is sometimes all we feel we need: "I was ready to be a better person than I had ever been before," a former nun in Mother Teresa's order writes in her memoir, "and all Mother had done was walk through the door" (Johnson 2012, p. 22).

We tend to exaggerate the leader's role as a bringer of solutions, and make celebrities of people in leadership roles – then dismiss them when they fall short. Even those who study leadership tend to turn it into a romance, with the leader – if authentic enough, or compassionate enough, or visionary enough, or resilient enough – cast as the vital figure who brings unity, imparts wisdom, and leads the group to safety and vitality (Gutmann (2023) criticizes this tendency as the "action fallacy"). Mostly we realize this is a fantasy: leaders are people just like us, with the same frailties and limits – and with even greater space for indulgence of ego, creative mischief, and self-dealing. So the experience of leadership in our lives is fraught: it is a mode of problem-solving that can unleash even greater problems. Perhaps it is coincidental, but perhaps not, that at this moment, as problems mount, so many people around the world, including in the mightiest nation that has ever existed, have lost confidence in the slow, uneven, often impersonal progress of modern democratic-bureaucratic govern-ance, and have turned their hearts instead to boastful bearers of simple solutions. These would-be redeemers promise, if they are given power unchecked by limit or accountability, a return to old certainties, purified identities, and the restored greatness of the group.

To help untangle this knot of perplexities, let's tease out one thread, a fragment of an old leadership story. Twenty centuries ago, when the new Christian faith was little more than a loose group of bickering religious entre-preneurs and fragile proto-churches perched in hostile or indifferent communi-ties, one of the early leaders, Paul, set out to convert non-Jews to the new religion. On an early mission, according to Acts of the Apostles in the New Testament, he came to Philippi, a Greco-Roman city in modern-day Greece. He preached, proselytized, and baptized a few believers. But who actually built the church at Philippi? According to the Bible, it was a woman named Lydia.

Lydia appears in just a couple of lines in Acts, a work of uncertain veracity and historicity. She was, the text suggests, an unmarried or widowed woman of business in the textile or dyeing trade, not a native of Philippi but Thyatira, a town about 200 miles to the east (Ascough 2009). She was apparently not a Jew but a Gentile, a "God-worshipper" or "God-fearer" in the language of the era – a pagan who was drawn to the lean and imposing monotheism of Judaism's Yawheh without embracing the rituals and culture of the Jewish religion. In Philippi, Paul preached and baptized new believers, including Lydia. Afterward she invited Paul and his companions to her household. Paul stayed in her house before going to preach in the city, where he was soon jailed. After miraculously escaping, he returned to her house and spoke to new converts there, before moving on to his next mission. Lydia stayed, and got to work.

In answer to Peter Drucker's question for leaders – "What needs to be done?" – Lydia would have had a lot to do: oversee a collaborative effort to proselytize, welcome, and educate new believers; organize the growing church;

collect and spend revenues; manage meetings; write letters; settle doctrinal disputes; arrange for baptism; tend to the sick among the congregation; bring food to the poor; conduct funerals for the dead; and find appropriate worship and meeting spaces as the church grew. The social and political setting was dynamic and dangerous: she would have had to hold her community together against competition from other mystery faiths, messianic sects, and charismatic movements; guard it against the suspicion and hostility of Jews and pagans; and seek to avoid or survive prosecution and imprisonment by the Roman civil authorities. And we can be sure there were those in Philippi who thought of themselves as good and loyal Christ-followers but doubted that Lydia, or perhaps any woman, was the right leader for the job, so that she had to put energy into explaining her judgments and actions, public relations, fence-mending, building alliances, winning votes or at least consent in gatherings of members of the community, and facing down challenges to her authority.

We don't know how long Lydia remained leader of the startup Philippian church. The pattern of female church leadership in Philippi may have held for some years, for in a subsequent letter to the Philippians, Paul tries to smooth a doctrinal conflict between two women, Euodia and Syntyche – seemingly the leaders of the congregation, for no one other member is named.[2] And it is noteworthy that this church seems to have played an exceptional role in supporting the mission work of Paul, according to his letter:

> You yourselves also know, Philippians, that at the first preaching of the gospel, after I left Macedonia, no church shared with me in the matter of giving and receiving except you alone; for even in Thessalonica you sent a gift more than once for my needs. (Phil. 4:15–16, NASB)[3]

As long as the early church was a collection of energetic spiritual entrepreneurs, exciting new visions, and passionate mini-movements, unexpected figures like Lydia could emerge in leadership roles by sheer force of conviction, personality, and opportunity. But soon enough Christianity hardened into a set of rival churches, burgeoning bureaucracies, and patriarchal ideologies that crowded out women as potential leaders. Centuries later Lydia was still remembered, but in a way that diminished her achievement: not as a leader but as Saint Lydia, the first documented 'European' (as that term came to be used) convert to Christianity. Lydia the leader was rediscovered by American women's rights

---

[2] The influential King James translation of the Bible (1611) replaced Euodia's name with the masculine form, Euodias. On Euodia and Syntyche as leaders, see Fellows and Stewart (2018).

[3] Unless otherwise noted, quotations from the Bible are from the New American Standard Bible (NASB).

advocates in the nineteenth century, notably Harriet Beecher Stowe in her 1873 book *Woman in Sacred History*.

Lydia's story, as faint as its traces may be, reveals something vital about leadership. Unlike bureaucratic office or customary authority, the essence of leadership is creative: a moment of opportunity and initiative that a human being steps into. Leaders help groups solve problems in creative ways. When the answers provided by formal or traditional authority don't do the job, anyone can ask, "What needs to be done?" Usually there will be no sustained response from others, so most leadership sparks fail to catch fire. Lydia's leadership story is fascinating not simply because she succeeded in building a church in a time when few women were accepted as leaders, but because she did so in a situation of radical innovation and uncertainty: a new faith, a new way of understanding human identity, a church arising out of Judaism but rejecting Jewish tradition, no past authority, no rules, no customs to provide guidance – only occasional correspondence and visits with other fledgling churches, and the rare letter (and one more visit, years later) from Paul. The novelty of the situation meant that Lydia had to begin by asking some basic questions about the nature and purpose of this new community, and how it could endure. Asking by itself wasn't enough – she also had to figure out answers, and turn them into effective action. But Lydia's work began with questions.

Leadership, according to the main modern Western tradition, is about influence and persuasion, collaboration, and results. But before all that, it's about wrestling with questions. This is not a unique insight – indeed, it's a recurring theme in thoughtful approaches to leadership from Plato to Peter Drucker. "One can lead," as Ron Heifetz and Donald Laurie concluded an influential article, "with no more than a question in hand" (1997, p. 78). Leadership helps solve problems through critical inquiry that sparks creative solutions. If the problems facing a group are simple, familiar, or not time-urgent, then the group has no great need for leadership. It can rely on its rules, systems, routines, traditions, accumulated knowledge, and capacity for incremental adaptation. Or the problem can simply remain unresolved. But when something urgent has happened, so that the old answers and ways of solving problems no longer provide suitable results, or problems pile up to a breaking point, the group enters a critical phase, and now it needs new answers. Thus it, or someone at least, needs to ask questions.

But can't anyone ask? Why link questions to leaders? Yes, it is true that anyone can ask, and all sorts of questions occur to all sorts of people. Indeed, the spark of leadership is universal, and latent in every individual. A surprising number of people of all different kinds could lead very well, if given the opportunity. But to ask a question that draws attention to a problem is risky. It is the recognized leader of a group who has the most freedom to ask questions, to create space for others' questions, and to make inquiry an accepted norm. Without a leader's example and support, the space for questions shrinks (Edmondson 2018).

A question-based definition of leadership risks making leaders sound like philosophers, and we're used to thinking of philosophy as impractical, removed from the urgency of groups struggling to survive and flourish. But there's no gainsaying it. Leadership *is* philosophical. It is a special kind of philosophy: applied or practical wisdom to help people in groups navigate the world effectively. The Greeks had a word for it: phronesis.[4] Happily, phronesis, or practical wisdom, does not belong to philosophers or leaders, but to all of us: we are all everyday philosophers – or can be, especially with a bit of education in critical thinking (for phronesis in business school education, for instance, see Amann and Goh 2017). Embracing your capacity to ask questions is the first step toward leadership in your own life.

In the sections that follow we'll explore what goes into the practical wisdom of leadership. Section 2 surveys some of the main traditions of thinking about leadership, noting the enduring importance of questions and inquiry. Section 3 looks at the human space where leadership happens, the group, and the existential questions that help shape its life. Section 4 looks at how culture and bureaucracy serve to provide stable answers to these questions. Section 5 looks at the very different way that leadership offers disruptive answers, especially in times of change and crisis. Section 6 concludes our exploration by considering not the leader but the group, and the question we all ask, 'What about us?' A Plutarchian coda uses the lens of questions to consider two parallel American lives, President Abraham Lincoln and General Robert E. Lee.

2 Traditions of Leadership Inquiry

> All of the great leaders have had one characteristic in common: it was the willingness to confront unequivocally the major anxiety of their people in their time. This, and not much else, is the essence of leadership.
>
> *John Kenneth Galbraith (1977, p. 330)*

---

[4] See for instance Plato's Meno, and especially Book VI of Aristotle's *Nicomachean Ethics*. The traditional Latin translation of phronesis was *prudentia*. Many translators of the *Nicomachean Ethics* maintain a continuity with past translations by rendering the word as "prudence" – for instance, Robert Bartlett and Susan Collins (Aristotle 2011). Joe Sachs, by contrast, renders the word as "practical judgment" in his translation (Aristotle 2002). He argues in his glossary that the English word 'prudence' "has connotations of caution that Aristotle did not intend" (in Aristotle 2002, p. 209). Whatever translation one uses, phronesis signifies, in Aristotle's works especially, a communal perspective, not solely an individual one: "Aristotle maintains that phronesis involves an understanding of the human good as a whole ... with the aim of doing well" (Russell 2014, p. 205). Phronesis is a good word for thinking about the wisdom and skills of leadership. (It is also the name of an excellent podcast by the leadership scholar Scott J. Allen.)

People have wondered and worried about leadership for a very long time. The oldest known literary work is an inquiry into the nature of leadership: the epic of the legendary king Gilgamesh, which dates back forty or more centuries to Mesopotamia, where some of the world's first cities arose. The epic is the story of the education of an imperfect and all-too-human leader. The question it poses is still pertinent today: can anything be done about a leader who doesn't love his people? Initially Gilgamesh, a gigantic, part-divine man of raging appetites, is an uncaring despoiler of the people of his city, Uruk. The people pray to the gods for some sort of solution and in response the gods send Enkidu, a powerful wild man. Enkidu is almost as strong as Gilgamesh, a new experience for the king. They wrestle and become fast friends. For the first time in his life Gilgamesh experiences emotional closeness, love, and vulnerability. But Enkidu gets sick and dies, and Gilgamesh now tastes grief, fear, and loneliness. He becomes obsessed with his own death ("Must I die too? Must Gilgamesh be like that?" (Ferry 1992, p. 48)) and sets out on a quest for immortality. He overcomes dangers, experiences mysteries, gains secret knowledge, and is finally guided to a magic plant, "How-the-Old-Man-Once-Again-Becomes-a-Young-Man" (p. 80). He has it in his grasp, but loses it. At the end, in his lowest moment, returning to his city alone and defeated, having gained nothing but some knowledge of the mysterious world beyond his kingdom, he comes into view of his city.

Now the story reaches its unexpected lesson. Gilgamesh gazes on the beautiful cultivated fields, the gardens, the walls, and the whole city of Uruk, seeing it from the outside as if for the first time: a whole community, a precious little world. Some of the poem's last lines echo some of the opening lines ("Study the brickwork, study the fortification / climb the great ancient staircase to the terrace; / study how it is made; from the terrace see / the planted and fallow fields, the ponds and orchards"). The poem's structure suggests that a great circle has closed, that Gilgamesh's vision has deepened, and that while this city endures, the leader who helped build and sustain it has some claim to immortality. Call it the consolation of leadership, to help build something that survives beyond a human life – and, also, to accept wonder and mystery into one's experience of life (Harvey 2008). The Gilgamesh story reveals an eternal tension in the authority of those who seek to lead – does their authority rest on their own skill and power, or in some degree of acceptance or consent by the community? And the poem suggests that the full measure of a leader includes their curiosity and capacity to learn new things.

Many other early texts grapple with leadership and authority. An ancient Sumerian proverb wryly observes, "You can have a king and you can have a lord, but the man to fear is the tax collector" (Scott 2017, p. 140). The Egyptian *Maxims of Ptahhotep* is a 44-century-old handbook of appropriate conduct for the ruling classes that reads like it was written by a veteran court official who's seen it all: "Do not repeat slander, / And do not listen to it, / For it is but the prattling of a churlish man. ... Suppress your impulses and control your mouth, / And then your advice will be (welcomed) by the officials" (Simpson 2003, pp. 140, 147).

In the Jewish Torah, Moses learns to delegate, showing himself capable of listening to advice from another man (Jethro, the world's first management consultant, Exodus 18), and King David learns that kings are not exempt from the moral codes others live by (2 Samuel 12). One of the most striking leadership moments in the Torah occurs when God threatens to wipe out the Israelites and Moses, in perhaps the first written instance of 'managing up' (Ashford and Detert 2015), talks his boss out of it with the clever use of questions:

> Lord, why does Your anger burn against Your people whom You have brought out from the land of Egypt with great power and with a mighty hand? Why should the Egyptians talk, saying, 'With evil motives He brought them out, to kill them on the mountains and to destroy them from the face of the earth'? Turn from Your burning anger and relent of doing harm to Your people. (Exod. 32:10–12)

Such an impulsive action, Moses' questions make clear, will make other peoples doubt Jehovah. As for Moses himself, the people he is attempting to lead to the promised land repeatedly challenge his leadership by asking sharp questions:

> Who made you a ruler and a judge over us? (Exod. 2:14)

> Is it because there were no graves in Egypt that you have taken us away to die in the wilderness? Why have you dealt with us in this way, bringing us out of Egypt? Is this not the word that we spoke to you in Egypt, saying, "Leave us alone that we may serve the Egyptians"? (Exod. 14:11–2)

> Is it a fact that the Lord has spoken only through Moses? Has He not spoken through us as well? (Num. 12:2).

> You have gone too far! The whole community is holy, every one of them, and the Lord is with them. Why then do you set yourselves above the Lord's assembly? (Num. 16:3, NIV)

These questions are tolerated for a while, but eventually lead to divine punishment. A similar dynamic operates in the Book of Job, which could also be called the book of questions: Job asks God more than 100 questions centered on trying to understand the nature of human suffering. God, when he finally responds, hurls back dozens of rhetorical questions that assert his power:

> Now tighten the belt on your waist like a man;
> I will ask you, and you instruct Me.
> Will you really nullify My judgment?
> Will you condemn Me so that you may be justified?
> Or do you have an arm like God,
> And can you thunder with a voice like His? *(Job 40:7–9)*

God's response to Job's questions is "an overwhelming series of questions intended to belittle Job – to crush him into insignificance by virtue of his being a mere man" (Gabel and Wheeler 1990, p. 116). The text ends with Job's questions silenced rather than answered: "The book offers no satisfactory answer to the agonizing query, the shortest question of all, 'Why?' " (Crenshaw 1992, vol. 3, p. 862; for a broad study of politics in the Hebrew Bible, see Walzer 2012).

In the New Testament, the contest between Jesus and the Jewish priestly classes, the Pharisees and Sadducees, that plays out in the synoptic gospels is essentially a theatrical battle of questions performed before a fascinated public. Each side deploys seemingly unanswerable questions meant to baffle or trap the other side:

> The chief priests and the elders of the people came to Him while He was teaching, and said, "By what authority are You doing these things, and who gave You this authority?" But Jesus responded and said to them, "I will also ask you one question, which, if you tell Me, I will also tell you by what authority I do these things. The baptism of John was from what source: from heaven or from men?" And they began considering the implications among themselves, saying, "If we say, 'From heaven,' He will say to us, 'Then why did you not believe him?' But if we say, 'From men,' we fear the people; for they all regard John as a prophet." And answering Jesus, they said, "We do not know." He also said to them, "Neither am I telling you by what authority I do these things." (Matt. 21:23–27)

The battle finally ends when Jesus overwhelms his adversaries with yet one more hard question. "No one was able to offer Him a word in answer, nor did anyone dare from that day on to ask Him any more questions" (Matt. 22:46). Jesus' ability to pose knotty questions whose answers required a creative leap only he could make was a vital element of his charismatic appeal. One of the lessons of the Bible is that questions have power, and asking too many can be dangerous.

China has one of the world's oldest traditions of leadership exploration, a good deal of it centered on the persistent encouragement of leader-rulers to subordinate their interests, or at least ego, to the group. The Chinese *Daode*

Jing, for example, credited to Laozi and written about 400 BCE, presents a view of leadership that stresses humility, connection, and circumspection (Laozi 2005, p. 37):

> When leaders do not trust enough,
>   they are themselves not trusted.
> When they are quiet and choose their words with care,
>   they accomplish all their tasks, achieve their goals,
> and everybody says, "Look at what we've done ourselves."

Another Chinese ethical tradition, Confucianism, stretches back to at least the sixth century BCE. A rich humanistic set of teachings, Confucianism (or Ruism) emphasizes the importance of piety, loyalty, and the ruler's wisdom and benevolence (see Ma and Tsui 2015). The legacy of Confucian thought was employed in complex ways, sometimes to foster obedience, sometimes to resist immoral or destructive leadership behavior. Near the end of the Ming dynasty in the seventeenth century, for instance, the scholar and reformer Huang Zongxi used his study of the Confucian tradition to criticize the authoritarian dynasty (Huang 1993).

In India's literary heritage there are many texts that explore leadership. The two-millennia-old Sanskrit treatise *Arthashastra* (*The Science of Material Gain*), traditionally credited to Kautilya, provides advice for leaders on statecraft, economics, and military strategy. It is coldly realistic, often described as anticipating a Machiavellian perspective on leadership and politics (Ramaswamy 2007; see also Boesche 2003). Another enduring text from the same era is the Bhagavad Gita (*Song of God*), a dialogue between a young prince and his charioteer teacher, aimed at the moral education of the young leader. The Bhagavad Gita considers the ethics of war and the importance of self-awareness, empathy, principled action, and ongoing spiritual development for leaders (Davis 2015).

A rich vein of leadership exploration appears in fifth- and fourth-century BCE Greek texts, especially the histories of Herodotus, plays by Sophocles, Euripides, and others, the dialogues of Plato, and the works of Aristotle. Plato's Socrates, always in conversation with others, seeks to uncover the nature of the *technē* or craft of leadership, and insists that at the heart of good leadership is a moral understanding of the leader's work. A debate plays out in Plato's works between his Socrates, wryly persistent about the moral imperatives of leadership or statesmanship, and the professional teachers of rhetoric like Thrasymachus, who assert that leadership is a collection of skills that can be packaged, taught, and used for any purpose. Plato's Socrates is keenly aware of the utility of leadership skills. As he says in the *Republic*, the dialectic, the art of asking questions, is the most dangerous skill one can teach intelligent young people (*Republic* 537d–541b). But he insists (most power-fully by the example of his own life and death) that a leader or citizen has a duty to serve the common good, and that this duty includes hard thinking, honest speaking, and patient curiosity to hear others' perspectives (see Stone 1988, Vlastos 1991, and Taylor 1998). Paul Woodruff characterizes Socrates' approach as "a way of thinking characterized by discontent with easy answers" (1998, p. 26).

The playwright Sophocles also contributed to the ancient Greeks' exploration of leadership, for instance in *Antigone*, where a young woman defies her uncle, the new ruler of Thebes, about the proper burial of her brother. The stubborn insistence of old man and young woman that each is right and the other wrong – a classic instance of what Rushworth Kidder calls a clash of "right versus right" – has tragic consequences for their family, and their city (2005, p. 86; see also Badger 2013).

Half a millennium after Socrates, around the end of the first century CE, another Greek writer, Plutarch, wrote a set of forty-eight 'parallel lives' that compared famous leaders from Greek and Roman history and legend: founders like Theseus and Romulus, lawgivers like Lycurgus and Numa Pompilius, kings, tyrants, reformers, demagogues, and generals. He emphasized the moral character of his subjects as a key to understanding their lives, successes, and failures. His works were influential for many centuries, particularly in the eastern, Greek half of the Roman Empire, and were reintroduced into Europe in the fifteenth century, where they became abidingly popular. Four of Shakespeare's plays – *Julius Caesar*, *Antony and Cleopatra*, *Timon of Athens*, and the extraordinary *Coriolanus* ("every political scientist's favorite play," the political scientist Ted Lowi once remarked) – draw from Plutarch, via Thomas North's 1579 English translation (Pelling 2002).

After Christianity became the official religion of the Roman Empire in the fourth century, perspectives on leadership became increasingly Christianized, as in St. Augustine's praise of the emperor Constantine in the fifth-century *City of God* (Augustine 1986, pp. 220–221). Until the end of the Middle Ages, the 'Mirror of Princes' was the leading genre of European leadership instruction, intended to help and encourage rulers to govern according to Christian virtues. In his *Speculum Regum* (*Mirror of Kings*), for instance, the twelfth-century chronicler, poet, and diplomat Godfrey of Viterbo drew leadership lessons from classical texts, biblical sources, and contemporary politics. There was a similar Muslim tradition of books of statecraft and advice for rulers, like the *Seyāsat-nāmeh* (*Rules for Kings*) by the eleventh-century Persian scholar and vizier Niẓām al-Mulk (Boroujerdi 2013; Marlow 2023).

The modern 'scientific' approach to the study of leadership is often said to begin with Niccolò Machiavelli, the sixteenth-century Florentine historian, writer, and civil servant. The claim is overblown. For one, there had been pragmatic thinking about leadership before Machiavelli. The Indian thinker Kautilya, for instance, mentioned earlier, or the twelfth-century Muslim scholar Ibn Ẓafar al-Ṣiqillī (Dekmejian and Thabit 2000) or even Aristotle, in his willingness in Book V of the *Politics* to explore how a tyrant could succeed (for a modern revisiting of this theme, see Dikötter 2019). And Machiavelli himself was less a scientist than a passionate poet and talented playwright who idealized the Roman republic, brooded over the weakness of the Italian rulers of his day, and yearned for a strong leader to unite Italy (Sullivan 2000). Machiavelli's thought was deeply misogynistic; he contributed to the enduring view that the role of leader is inherently a masculine one, in particular a masculinity centered in violence, lonely distrust, and cold cognition (see Hanna Pitkin's (1984) brilliant exploration, *Fortune Is a Woman*). But Machiavelli's audacious analysis of leadership behavior, centered on the question of what works, was influential in shifting thinking about leadership away from "ought" and toward "is." In *The Prince*, for instance, he says, "This has to be understood: that a prince, and especially a new prince, cannot observe all those things for which men are held good, since he is often under a necessity, to maintain his state, of acting against faith, against charity, against humanity, against religion" (Machiavelli 1985, p. 70). His popular legacy – not an incorrect one – is as an amoral teacher of the dark arts of leadership, including violence and deception. Thoughtful readers also take note of other aspects of his thought, including his preference for republics over princedoms and his consistent advice that the long-term success of a leader depends on avoiding hatred and making the community secure. The enduring measure of a leader, Machiavelli said, is the well-being of the people (Cosans and Reina 2018). To be effective, Machiavelli urged would-be leaders to guard against the lies of flatterers, train themselves to look past surface appearances, and question everything.

The stirrings of industry, commerce, science, and exploration in Europe from about the fourteenth and fifteenth centuries onward began to change how people thought about leadership. Many began to pay less attention to the actions or the virtue of rulers, and more attention to interactions among people. Thomas Hobbes and John Locke in the seventeenth century and Jean-Jacques Rousseau in the eighteenth century developed the idea of the social contract as the idealized basis of political authority. Adam Smith made a similar argument about economics, arguing that the best way to support human flourishing was by the "invisible hand" of a myriad of individual preferences and choices, rather than the heavy hand of regulation, tradition, or a ruler's caprice (Smith 1759, part IV, ch. 1; 1776, Book IV, ch. 2). The American founders established the new government with an emphasis on structure rather than selecting or educating the right leaders. In *Federalist 51* (1788), James Madison, the new constitution's chief architect, explained its almost mechanical working: the trick was "contriving the interior structure of the government as that its several constituent parts may, by their mutual relations, be the means of keeping each other in their proper places" (Hamilton, Madison, and Jay 1961, p. 320). Even for the people who would act within this structure, the thinking was structural and impersonal: "Ambition must be made to counteract ambition. The interest of the man must be connected with the constitutional rights of the place" (p. 322). Madison concluded on a philosophical note:

> It may be a reflection on human nature, that such devices should be necessary to control the abuses of government. But what is government itself, but the greatest of all reflections on human nature? If men were angels, no government would be necessary. If angels were to govern men, neither external nor internal controls on government would be necessary. (p. 322; see also Weaver 1997)

The new emphasis on rights, rules, and roles, as uncertain and hypocritical it was in its implementation (and it was very much so), revealed to some the situation of those who lacked rights altogether. In England, Mary Wollstonecraft argued in her *Vindication of the Rights of Woman* (1792) that women had the right to live independent lives, attain education, and find meaningful work in the world. She did not explicitly address women's leadership: "I do not wish them to have power over men; but over themselves" (1992, p. 156). But the logic of a woman's potential for leadership was clear: "Can she believe that she was only made to submit to man, her equal?" (p. 162). It would take a long time for that logic to be widely accepted.[5]

At about the same time as Wollstonecraft's book, the leaders of the Haitian revolt against French colonial rule wrote a letter to the French Assembly General: "For too long we have borne your chains without thinking of shaking them off, but any authority which is not founded on virtue and humanity, and which only tends to subject one's fellow man to slavery, must come to an end" (Bell 2007, p. 40). The Haitian Revolution was a unique historical achievement, the only revolt by enslaved people that succeeded in establishing a free state. But France imposed a bitter settlement. Haiti, ironically and tragically, "became the world's first and only country where the descendants of enslaved people paid

---

[5] The most recent American milestone of gender equality in business leadership shows how far there is still to go: in 2023, for the first time, the percentage of Fortune 500 companies led by women exceeds 10 percent (Hinchliffe 2023). For an overview, see Goethals and Hoyt (2017).

reparations to the descendants of their masters – for generations" (Porter, Méheut, Apuzzo, and Gebrekidan 2022). Haiti's colonial legacy left it, after more than a century of 'reparations' debt repayment, the poorest country in the Western Hemisphere, with very low civic pride and trust in governance and leaders (Gélineau, Montalvo and Schweizer-Robinson 2021, esp. ch. 5).

Across the world, European colonialism (supported or replicated in some places by American power) devastated native peoples and how they practiced and perceived authority and leadership. In Africa, for example, the immensity of colonialism in the nineteenth century shattered traditional authority patterns. This cataclysm of upheaval was explored by the Nigerian writer Chinua Achebe in novels like *Things Fall Apart* (1958), *Arrow of God* (1964), and *A Man of the People* (1966) (see Okolo 2007 and Gosling 2013, as well as Section 4). Today, a range of thinkers seeks to preserve or recover African understandings of governance and leadership. Traditional African explorations of leadership are primarily oral, and with thousands of different cultures across the African continent, it is hard to generalize. Still, a few themes tend to emerge: communalism and kinship, the past connected to the present, and a multiplicity of leadership and authority roles (a council of elders rather than a single strong ruler, for instance). A central concept in many traditions of African political and leadership thought can be conveyed by the term *Ubuntu*, a Nguni Bantu term meaning 'humanity,' 'humaneness,' or 'human connectedness' (Menkiti 1984; Ramose 1999; Etieyibo and Ikuenobe 2020).

Among the indigenous peoples of the Americas, a similar pattern of communalism rather than individual leadership was common. Among the Muscogee (Creek) Indians, originally of the southeast, now located mainly in Oklahoma, "leaders wielded authority only as long as they could persuade others to agree with their decisions" (Frank n.d.) Similarly, among the Wendat people of the northeast, the anthropologists David Graeber and David Wengrow relate, "an office holder could give all the orders he or she liked, but no one was under any particular obligation to follow them" (2021, p. 43). Among the Xavante hunter-gatherers of Brazil, there is intense competition to become a leader, but once achieved, that aggressive energy must be transformed into something more communal:

> A Xavante chief ... walks a tightrope. In order to be recognized as a chief, he must be passionate, competitive, even ruthless. However, once he has achieved that status he is referred to as a watchman, a man who looks over and looks after his community, and then he needs to be a mediator and builder of consensus. Otherwise his community will break up, people will move away, and the very basis of his authority will be undermined. (Maybury-Lewis 1992, p. 237)

Graeber and Wengrow observe that while indigenous societies in the Americas had many different modes of living, they tended to be freer and more humane than settler societies. Indeed, it was Europeans' contact with the indigenous cultures of the Americas, they provocatively argue, that helped spark the Enlightenment's 'new' ideas about freedom and equality (2021, pp. 48–56). Looking at indigenous societies around the world, anthropologist Jeffrey Sissons asserts that indigenous thought has preserved an old approach to leadership and political authority:

> At the heart of all indigenous cultures are relations between kin that differ profoundly from the ways that kin relations are practiced and understood in settler cultures. Kinship in most indigenous cultures includes an ongoing relationship with the land and natural environment, for example, an understanding that is entirely absent from settler cultures that originated in Europe. This indigenous understanding of kinship extends from cosmology to political and economic life and provides a foundation for cultural resistance to the rational operation of state power within post-settler states. ... Kinship cosmologies and kin-based polities do not sit easily with systems based on bureaucratic rationality. (Sissons 2005, p. 33)[6]

But bureaucratic rationality has steadily gained power in the modern world. While the leader of modernity may have greater power than leaders in the past, thanks to complex systems of governance, commerce, and technology, the modern leader is more managerial, more hemmed in by bureaucratic modes of control. One notable reaction within the Western tradition against this bureaucratization of leadership came from the nineteenth-century Scottish writer Thomas Carlyle, who expounded the view that history was made not by forces and institutions, but in fact by 'heroes' – a few individuals who possessed extraordinary qualities (Carlyle 2013). Carlyle's Romantic 'great man' view of history caught the popular imagination and remains a common starting point for leadership textbooks today.

Scholars, however, prefer to study leadership contextually, especially within the social science disciplines that formalized around the end of the nineteenth century. Each of the social sciences – political science, anthropology, sociology, psychology, and management – emphasizes certain aspects of leadership. Political science studies leadership within frameworks of the state, legislation, interest groups, parties, influence, decision-making, and administration.

---

[6] The New Zealand writer Witi Ihimaera beautifully explores this cluster of themes as they affect the people in a struggling Maori village in his novel *The Whale Rider* (1987). Ihimaera's novel imagines strong indigenous leadership even while inverting some of its cultural expectations, like the possibility of a young girl being the leader. Niki Caro's 2002 film version, *Whale Rider*, is equally powerful.

A political scientist of the nineteenth century, Woodrow Wilson (well before he became the 28th American president) surveyed American politics and saw only confusion: "this multiplicity of leaders, this many-headed leadership," that produced a "disconnected and therefore unsystematic, confused, and desultory action" (Wilson 1900, p. 61). From the political science perspective the stunning rise of Donald Trump to the American presidency is less a Carlylean 'great man' story than a variation on the familiar workings of populism (Howell and Moe 2020; Harvey 2022).

Another social science, anthropology, studies human communities in the past and present, with special attention to their cultures. At the start of the twentieth century the anthropologist Franz Boas developed the concept of cultural relativism, which held that a genuine effort to understand a culture must occur within, not outside, that culture's perspective. Another influential anthropologist, Claude Lévi-Strauss, helped develop an understanding of the weak leadership typical of hunter-gatherer groups. Today the subfield of evolutionary anthropology emphasizes the study of small, politically autonomous communities, most long-vanished, to better understand how the workings of leadership developed over hundreds of thousands of years of human existence (Garfield, von Rueden, and Hagen 2019). Sociology, the study of how people live and interact in modern groups, organizations, and societies, yields insight through research on social beliefs, authority and legitimacy, stratification, inequality, institutions, change, deviance, crime and punishment, and bureaucracy. All of these shape the space within which leadership phenomena happen (Venkatesh 2008).

The discipline that has most significantly shaped the modern study of leadership is psychology. Most of the cited research in leadership studies is from psychology. Psychologists study group and intra-group dynamics, influence processes, individual traits, interpersonal dynamics, and pertinent phenomena like charisma, followership, motivation, perception, bias, communication, attribution, and more. One durable discussion stimulated by research in psychology, for instance, is whether leadership is best understood as a role or an influence process (Yukl 2010, p. 3). In recent decades the subfield of evolutionary psychology, similar to evolutionary anthropology, has turned more attention to the possible evolutionary origins of some of these aspects of life in groups (van Vugt and Ronay 2014; Stewart-Williams 2018).

Management, which only arose as a distinct field of study in the twentieth century, has also contributed a great deal to the study of leadership. A pioneering thinker was Henri Fayol, a French mining engineer and manager. "To manage," Fayol wrote in the field's first serious work, *General and Industrial Management*, "is to plan, organize, coordinate, command, and control" (1987 [1916], p. 13; see also Parker and Ritson 2005). After Fayol, generations of business students studied "the functions of management." Another influential twentieth-century figure in the study of management was Peter Drucker, whose work encouraged a synthesis of research, observation, humanistic attention to the well-being and growth of workers, and philosophical interest in the ethical imperatives of business leadership. Drucker's management books spanned six decades. In the introduction to one of his last books, he wrote, "management was neither my first nor has it been my foremost concern. I only became interested in it because of my work on community and society." His attention to business management, he said, was really an interest in "the corporation as *human effort* and as *social institution*" (Drucker 2003, p. vii, emphasis in the original).

As the case of Drucker suggests, the effort to make sense of leadership is best pursued as a hybrid or a dialogue of different approaches seeking to understand the human condition (Harvey and Riggio 2011). The study of leadership draws from all the social sciences, as well as history, ethics, imaginative literature, and ancient teachings and stories (Wren 1995; Riggio and Conger 2008; Ciulla 2014; Price 2008; McManus and Perruci 2020). Such richness of perspective has helped produce hundreds of definitions of leadership (Stogdill 1974, p. 259). But the situation is not as chaotic as it may seem, because definitions of leadership tend to aggregate around a few core elements: goals, an influence process, and collaborative action. Here, for instance, is a popular textbook definition by Gary Yukl:

> Leadership is the process of influencing others to understand and agree about what needs to be done and how to do it, and the process of facilitating individual and collective efforts to accomplish shared objectives. (2010, p. 8)

Today, the field of leadership studies accepts something like Yukl's definition as a guiding concept. Scholars add their own emphases, for instance authenticity – gaining and using influence by being true to yourself (George 2003; Avolio and Gardner 2005); charisma, by winning personal allegiance (House 1977; Conger, Kanungo, and Menon 2000), emotional intelligence, by monitoring and managing one's own and others' emotions (Mayer, Salovey, and Caruso 2004; Goleman, Boyatzis, and McKee 2004); spirituality, by drawing on and appealing to faith (Fry 2003; Reave 2005); and diversity, by challenging stereotypes of who can lead and increasing the pool of potential leaders (Hewlett, Luce, and West 2005; Austin and Pisano 2017; Fitzsimmons and Callan 2020).

All of these topics are worthy of exploration, but they tend to leave out a vital starting point: the exploration of "what needs to be done." Drucker's question is meant to spark the leader's endeavor. But grappling with it depends on answers to even more fundamental questions, at the heart of the human quest for meaning. These underlying questions are the true starting point of the leadership phenomenon, because they are where the group grounds its understanding and capacity for action.

3 The Group and Its Questions

As far as we can discern, the sole purpose of human existence is to kindle a light of meaning in the darkness of mere being.

Carl Jung (1963, p. 326)

Throughout human existence, we have lived in groups and worked collaboratively. "We are experts," the evolutionary anthropologist Brian Hare notes, "at working together with other people, even strangers. We can communicate with someone we've never met about a shared goal and work together to accomplish it. We develop this superpower before we can walk or talk, and it is the gateway to a sophisticated social and cultural world" (Hare and Woods 2020). Now, our heritage doesn't mean groups and collaboration are the measure of all things. Some people do their best work alone.[7] And evolution didn't just make us collaborative and social – it also made us individually calculating and strongly motivated to pursue our own self-interest. In addition, modern life pushes us steadily toward solitariness, so that we come to perceive being alone as normal, and increasingly seek substitutes for human companionship (Putnam 2000, Turkle 2012; for an exploration of the ethical aspects of some technological substitutes for loneliness, see Jecker 2021). Americans, for instance, now spend half their free time engaged in the solitary consumption of recreational experiences. But the increasing solitude of modern life comes at a cost; self-reported life satisfaction is negatively correlated with the amount of time spent alone (Atalay 2022).

Humans evolved to live and collaborate in groups because groups make us strong. Group-based collaboration is how we have solved our biggest problems. We toil together, fight together, build together, raise children together, dream together, mourn and rejoice together. Groups can undertake projects beyond the scope, strength, or wisdom of one person, with the division of labor giving many individuals useful roles to play. In groups the old or experienced can teach the young or inexperienced, specialists can hone their expertise, and lessons can be preserved and passed on that would otherwise be lost with each solitary

---

[7] See for instance Susan Cain's portrait of Apple's co-founder, Stephen Wozniak (Cain 2012, pp. 71–74). But note that Wozniak's enduring achievements came because his typically solitary work was part of an extraordinary collaborative effort with Steve Jobs and many other talented people.

lifespan. In the contemporary world, technology has advanced sufficiently to provide substitutes, in many situations, for these traditional functions of the group, but even technology still needs human groups for its conception, design, building, and deployment (Douglas 2023). It is truer than ever that groups, from startups to nations, shape our world – and even tilt its axis (Yarber 2023).

Although we evolved to live in groups, our past may have limits as a guidebook for today. Our species, *Homo sapiens*, is perhaps 300,000 years old. Our genus, *Homo* – a tangle of our ancestors and cousins – stretches back six or seven million years. For the vast majority of that time we and our ancestors lived in small groups of hunter-gatherers (but not in simple uniformity – see Arnold et al. 2016). Different ways of living – marked by agriculture and the domestication of animals, permanent settlements and urbanization, and the gradual integration of rapid technological innovation into our lives – have only arisen in the last 10,000 years old or so. And the pace of change has continued to increase, so that modern groups may simply be too different to bear much comparison with ancient ones. The anthropologists David Graeber and David Wengrow argue, for instance, that while "sceptics and non-conformists" have always existed in tension with groups, widespread antipathy to social structures and alienation are distinctly modern phenomena, associated with the relatively recent historical development of hierarchy and inequality (2021, p. 97). The upshot is that humans today live and toil very differently than our ancestors did in the past, and this change has been concentrated in a short, recent burst. Our ancestors, for instance, did not move from company to company or career to career: people generally were born into, lived and worked in, and died in groups that were both sites of material production and communities of families. Certainly the world of ancient human groups, considered over time, would show change, formation of new groups and decline and cessation of old ones, dispersal, movement, adaptation, and, again and again over a span of centuries and millennia, shocks and crises. But modern groups are far more transitory, provisional, subject to upheaval and reinvention on a short time scale, and limited by function. Family and economic work, for instance, have been separated for most people into different spheres of life. Modern groups have, at a level of abstraction, the same human dynamics as ancient ones – especially the need to get people working together on common projects – but modern groups are thinner, and people tend to have more choices about how to live, how to allocate their interests and passions, and which group to join or leave. One should be cautious about invoking the past to guide to how we should live and work today (Buchanan and Powell 2015).

But one can still step back and ask, conceptually if not historically, what it means to exist and endure as a group of human beings. (Recall that we define 'group' in this Element as two or more individuals sharing a purpose that requires interdependent work, with duration sufficient for habits and expectations to form.) Broadly, there are five big problems groups face. Four have to do with the group itself: its identity, its situation, its purpose, and its way of achieving that purpose. The fifth problem centers on the individual members of the group, and how they assess the costs and benefits of participation in the group. When solutions to these problems are perceived as reasonably effective and acceptable by group members, they are followed without much thought. But when one or more of the solutions stops working – perhaps something has changed in the group's situation – some people will do what comes naturally: notice, puzzle, and ask questions. The five problems of the group are, from another perspective, five questions – five existential questions – that underlie the group's life.

'Who Are We?'

The first question is deceptively simple: 'Who are we?' People new to leadership roles often understand that they should find out about the group's members, and this is a wise step in building leadership capacity. But 'Who are we?' is about more than the group's individual members – it's about the extent to which a group has a shared or a social identity (Haslam, Reicher, and Platow 2020). In part this is an empirical question that can be explored and answered factually. (The Old Testament's Book of Numbers, for instance, is called that because in it Moses orders two censuses of the Israelites to gauge their fighting strength.) But it is also a question that has a vital emotional and psychic dimension. 'Who we are' depends in large part on who we believe and feel we are. Nelson Mandela, in his majestic autobiography *Long Walk to Freedom*, recalls the confusion he felt as a young Xhosa man in the 1930s at his school, Healdtown, after hearing a poem performed by Krune Mqhayi, a famed Xhosa *imbongi* (a "praise-singer, . . . who marks contemporary events and history with poetry that is of special meaning to his people"):

> I did not want ever to stop applauding. I felt such intense pride at that point, not as an African, but as a Xhosa; I felt like one of the chosen people.
> I was galvanized, but also confused by Mqhayi's performance. He had moved from a more nationalistic, all-encompassing theme of African unity to a more parochial one addressed to the Xhosa people, of whom he was one. As my time at Healdtown was coming to an end, I had many new and sometimes conflicting ideas floating in my head. I was beginning to see that Africans of all tribes had much in common, yet here was the great Mqhayi praising the Xhosa above all. . . . In a sense, Mqhayi's shift in focus was a mirror of my

own mind because I went back and forth between pride in myself as a Xhosa and a feeling of kinship with other Africans. But as I left Healdtown at the end of the year, I saw myself as a Xhosa first and an African second. (Mandela 1995, pp. 40–41)

An answer to who we are also makes a statement of who we are *not*, which group we are not part of, or who is not part of our group. Shared social identity is a boundary or demarcation line around the group. Such boundaries make it easier to establish trust within the group, which facilitates collaboration. But they can also be drawn, not necessarily by the members of the group, to the detriment of both the group and individuals. The anthropologist Jeffrey Sissons calls this "oppressive authenticity," noting that in modern settler states like New Zealand, the United States, and Brazil, some indigenous people are deemed as not possessing the requisite cultural authenticity, in part because the definition of a "tribe" was formally demarcated by a colonial or post-colonial administration:

> British colonialism's most successful strategy, indirect rule, required offi-
> cially recognized leaders of bounded groups occupying fixed areas of land.
> Chiefs, tribes and mapped territories were among the essential conditions of
> empire. Once officially defined, these groups took on a 'traditional' authenti-
> city denied to other, 'non-tribal' groups that inhabited less clearly defined
> spaces. (Sissons 2005, p. 52)

'Who are we?' thus is a vital question for the group, and a psycho-emotional touchstone for its members – but also, at times, an exclusionary device that may be exploited by some within the group or by actors and forces beyond the group. It is a question that merits ongoing critical scrutiny.

'Where Are We?'

The second question is about understanding the world around the group. Humans, like all other species, adapt to particular environments, and deep knowledge about the environment is vital to a group's survival. For hunter-gatherer groups – the only groups that existed for more than 95 percent of our species' existence – this meant knowledge about the landscape, climate, terrain, bodies of water and the ways in which they are navigable or act as barriers, materials like flint or wood or peat available for exploitation, the eco-system and its food resources, habits and migrations of predators and prey, illnesses and remedies, the presence of neighboring groups, and more. Until just a few tens of thousands of years ago, neighboring groups might have included other human species, Neanderthals and Denisovans and *Homo floresiensis*. And we can be certain that our ancestors looked further than their immediate physical surroundings, to the heavens and horizons, wondering what was there, just out of sight, or appearing and reappearing every day, or every month, or every year. Some members of groups went on journeys, and some of these came back, and sometimes there were appearances by people from far away, distant kin or utter strangers. Their accounts and stories must have been eagerly received. Over time human groups devised lessons, myths, and beliefs about the whole world and their place in it.

For groups in the modern world (defined as the emergence of a capitalist economy in the last four or five centuries), the answer to the question of "Where are we?" also has an important abstract aspect, focused on the competitive environment in which the group exists. For modern groups this question is a basic strategic tool, taught to business students in thousands of classrooms around the world (typically as the second chapter of a strategic management textbook – see for instance Dess, McNamara, Eisner, and Sauerwald (2024). In this modern context the answers tend to focus less on physical situation, and more on understanding a specific industry or area of activity, with its particular constraints, challenges, and opportunities, its particular set of competitors and new entrants, and its rate of technological innovation and other kinds of change (Porter 1979).

'Where Are We Going?'

The first two questions, 'Who are we?' and 'Where are we?' are rooted in the present (and often reach back to the past). The third question, 'Where are we going?' is the great imaginative leap that humans are capable of – envisioning a world that does not yet exist, a place not yet reached. One might wonder whether humans and their groups truly need to ask this question. Cannot a group simply continue living as it has in the past? Certainly the timescale of change in the lives of our ancestral species – for instance in how they made stone tools – was unimaginably slow: the Oldowan knapping industry and its successor, the Acheulean, each lasted more than a million years. Only with the emergence of modern humans (*Homo sapiens* and our close cousins like the Neanderthals), starting about 300,000 years ago, did the pace of innovation increase. Change also comes to human lives from the pressure of the physical environment. Up until a few thousand years ago people flourished in places now under the oceans: Beringia (connecting Asia and North America across what is now the Bering Strait), Doggerland (connecting Great Britain and mainland Europe), Sundaland (connecting Indonesia to mainland Asia), and Sahul (connecting and encompassing Australia, Tasmania, New Guinea, and the Aru Islands). As the most recent Ice Age came to an end 12,000 years or so ago, these places were submerged by rising oceans (Spada and Galassi 2017). In all of these vanished lands, people once lived in what seemed like stability, until it wasn't.

Today, the question 'where are we going?' has daily urgency. Change buffets us on a scale and at a pace unimaginable to past peoples. Indigenous peoples, for instance, must figure out the best way to preserve their identity and culture, often by strategically embracing elements of change. The global capitalist economic system is incentivized for innovation and disruption. Culturally and politically, more and more people encounter new ideas, practices, and competitive pressures that call into doubt the wisdom or at least utility of old answers. Maintaining a long-standing group's traditional identity, values, and modes of existence in this whirlwind of change is extraordinarily difficult. Most groups – businesses, for instance, of course – have accepted the need for constant reinvention, redirection, and change of all kinds, so much so that innovation is often celebrated as a value in itself.

'How Do We Get There?'

"We campaign in poetry," the politician Mario Cuomo once said, "but when we're elected we're forced to govern in prose" (Carroll 1985, p. 26). If 'Where are we going?' is the poetic vision of a group, full of hope and possible futures, then the group's next big question, 'How do we get there?' is its practical prose, focused on what works in the here and now. At a critical moment in Steven Spielberg's movie *Lincoln* (2012), the president, still lacking votes in Congress and staring at the possible defeat of the Thirteenth Amendment, rallies his small team with a fierce vision:

> We're stepped out upon the world's stage now, now, with the fate of human dignity in our hands! Blood's been spilt to afford us this moment! Now now now! ... Abolishing slavery by constitutional provision settles the fate, for all coming time, not only of the millions now in bondage but of unborn millions to come. Two votes stand in its way, and these votes must be procured. (Kushner 2012, p. 128)

But one of his men, Congressman James Ashley, remains obdurate: "Yes but how?" (p. 128). Many soaring visions have crashed to earth because they couldn't find an answer to this simple question. Resistance to change is a powerful factor in the lives of groups. Machiavelli identified it as one of the leader's biggest challenges: "the innovator has for enemies all those who have done well under the old conditions, and lukewarm defenders in those who may do well under the new" (1985, p. 24). In many organizations, it's common to keep doing what you've been doing and wait for the tempest of change to blow over.

But there is a good reason that people tend to be skeptical or resistant about implementing answers in response to a call for significant change. A living group is a delicate thing. It has been fine-tuned to do something very well, over a longer period of time than is generally realized. No group is perfect, and it's often easier to notice the visible problems than the slowly gathered solutions and efficiencies. Translating a vision or plan for change into sustained positive results is extraordinarily difficult. An oft-repeated finding in the field of management is that most implementation efforts fail (Pryor, Anderson, Toombs, and Humphreys 2007, p. 3). The causes are many, but the short answer is that it's a lot easier to paint a vivid picture of an idealized destination than manage the innumerable details of getting the group there. A bold vision is often conceived and delivered by one person or a small team, but implementing the vision requires the labor of many people, carefully coordinated. If there tends to be widespread skepticism among people about leaders – and there is – it is in part due to the gap so often seen between the evoking of a bold plan and its feeble execution. The highest-profile example in recent American business history was the seventeen-month tenure of Ron Johnson, a marketing whiz at Apple, as a spectacularly unsuccessful CEO recruited by the struggling retailer J.C. Penney in 2011 (Reingold 2014).

By contrast, perhaps the greatest business example of a great implementer and master of 'how' is Alfred Sloan, who in the 1920s turned General Motors from a sprawling car company that had grown too rapidly into an intricately organized behemoth. In the process Sloan largely invented the divisionalized corporation. Two of his ideas are especially well known in management circles: "decentralization with co-ordinated control," and "a car for every purse and purpose" (1990, pp. 429, 441; see also Farber 2002).

'What about Me?'

The first four questions, squarely about 'us,' might seem to suggest that a group is an integrated collective with clear shared perspectives on identity, situation, and purpose. The fifth question – 'What about me?' – reminds us that this is more or less a fiction, or at least a flattening of reality. A group is a collection of individuals, and even as they collaborate, each makes calculations about the costs and benefits of participation, how much emotional energy to devote to the group, how much to trust it, and how deeply to identify and engage with it. Individuals form friendships and alliances within the group, but these may undermine rather than contribute to the group's collaborative capacity. Long ago the famed sociologist Erving Goffman described the opposing forces – "sense of being a person" versus "sense of selfhood" – pulling the individual in two directions, into the group and away from it:

> Perhaps we should ... defin[e] the individual, for sociological purposes, as a stance-taking entity, a something that takes up a position somewhere between identification with an organization and opposition to it, and is ready at the slightest pressure to regain its balance by shifting its involvement in either direction. ... Our sense of being a person can come from being drawn into a wider social unit; our sense of selfhood can arise through the little ways in which we resist the pull. (Goffman 1961, pp. 319–20)

The tension between the group and the individual – and, as Goffman observes, within the individual themself – is part of how groups work to shape shared human meanings. Each individual calculates, and may at any time recalculate, the degree of their connection to the group. Especially in the contemporary world, where we are members of many groups that touch our lives in different ways at different times, 'what about me?' is a question that is always active, or ready to be activated, for every member of the group.

Today we tend to think of groups narrowly, as instrumentalities for getting work done, with our membership defined by contract which in the main may be abrogated at any time by employer or employee. That is a prudent perspective in a capitalist world that relentlessly teaches us to define and guard our individual interests. But from another, equally true perspective, groups are the spaces in our lives where we come together to manifest our purpose in the world. An individual can find meaning and purpose in solitude.[8] But most human beings find their deepest experience of significance when they forge connections within a group that becomes, for them, a community. At its best, our shared life and work in a group, in helping us answer our deepest questions, can kindle a light of meaning in the darkness of mere being.

4 Stable Answers

> The white man is very clever. He came quietly with his religion. We were amused at his foolishness and allowed him to stay. Now he has won our brothers, and our clan can no longer act like one. He has put a knife on the things that held us together and we have fallen apart.
>
> *Chinua Achebe, Things Fall Apart (1994, p. 176)*

In our hearts, each of us asks questions about who we are, why we're here, and how we should live. Our individual answers, beautiful, shocking, or mundane, mostly live and die with us alone. At the level of groups, we have discovered just two ways of sharing and remembering answers to our deepest questions:

---

[8] Often by using solitude to reflect on their connections to other people and the world.

culture and bureaucracy. Culture is an evolutionary adaptation that draws on our species' highly developed cognitive and social learning skills (Marean 2015). It is as old as us. Bureaucracy is a recent contrivance, a set of (in principle) rationally derived and applied written rules. Culture also has rules, but they are unwritten. Both culture and bureaucracy can provide guidance and stable answers to groups. Let us consider them in turn, starting with a story about the fall of a mighty culture, the Igbo of southeastern Nigeria.

As a young Igbo college student in Nigeria in the early 1950s, Chinua Achebe read the novel *Mr. Johnson* in a class full of African students. It had been written in 1939 by the Anglo-Irish novelist and colonial official, Joyce Cary. Achebe's white teachers loved how the book, as they read it, humanized its Nigerian characters. The young Achebe was appalled: "it was clear to me that it was a most superficial picture of – not only of the country – but even of the Nigerian character and so I thought if this was famous, then perhaps someone ought to try and look at this from the inside" (Pieterse and Duerden 1972, p. 4). A few years later he wrote the novel that made him famous and inspired a renaissance and rediscovery of African literature by African writers.

Things Fall Apart dramatizes the overthrow of Igbo culture by British colonialism. It takes place in the 1890s, in the imagined village of Umuofia. The story follows the life of Okonkwo, famed as a wrestler and warrior among the Igbo people of the region. Driven by fear of ending up a failure like his father, he aspires to become one of the most respected and high-status men in the village, and is often violent to his wives, children, and others. Life in Umuofia is bound tightly by traditions, rituals, and pervasive belief in magic and spirits. When Okonkwo accidentally kills a teenage boy he is exiled for seven years, in accordance with custom. During his exile British missionaries and colonial administrators arrive in the village, bringing a strange religion and laws ("They had built a court where the District Commissioner judged cases in ignorance," p. 174). After his exile Okonkwo returns to his village, but he sees the changes and perceives a crisis. He resists the invaders by killing a colonial messenger and trying to rally an uprising, but when he realizes there will be no broader opposition he hangs himself. The novel ends with the District Commissioner arriving at the scene:

> "Take down the body," the Commissioner ordered his chief messenger, "and bring it and all these people to the court."
>
> "Yes, sah," the messenger said, saluting.
>
> The Commissioner went away, taking three or four of the soldiers with him. In the many years in which he had toiled to bring civilization to different parts of Africa he had learned a number of things. One of them was that a District Commissioner must never attend to such undignified details as

cutting a hanged man from the tree. Such attention would give the natives a poor opinion of him. In the book which he planned to write he would stress that point. As he walked back to the court he thought about that book. Every day brought him some new material. The story of this man who had killed a messenger and hanged himself would make interesting reading. One could almost write a whole chapter on him. Perhaps not a whole chapter but a reasonable paragraph, at any rate. There was so much else to include, and one must be firm in cutting out details. He had already chosen the title of the book, after much thought: *The Pacification of the Primitive Tribes of the Lower Niger.* (pp. 208–9)

Achebe's title comes from a couplet in W. B. Yeats' poem "The Second Coming," which Achebe makes the novel's epigraph: "Things fall apart; the center cannot hold; / Mere anarchy is loosed upon the world." The village of Umuofia, as strong it is has been – "feared by all its neighbors," "powerful in war and magic" (p. 11) – is the center that cannot hold. Its culture is overthrown by the colonizer, and its people's way of life is shattered.

Years later, Achebe explained his purpose: "The history of Africa is such that our business should be to restore what was lost. To take on the task of redefining ourselves" (Wachtel 1994). His novel helps us understand the power of Igbo culture, including how its essence was invisible to outsiders. His Commissioner, who plans to write a leadership advice book for colonial administrators, has nothing of value to teach because he has understood nothing.

What is culture? It is a "shared collective meaning system" that represents a group's "collective values, attitudes, beliefs, customs, and thoughts" (Barnett and Lee 2002, p. 277). Some manifestations of culture are easy to perceive: the ways people dress and decorate themselves, their language, their art, their food, their homes and other structures and spaces, the performance of ceremonies and rituals. Culture is also expressed in the group's shared stories, in its proverbs and sayings, in speeches, sermons, and other public utterances, in sacred or revered texts, in lessons for the young. Deepest of all, culture is a set of beliefs about how the world works, what the group's place is in the world, how people (including often different categories of people) should behave and be treated and regarded in the group, and what is needed for the group to endure and flourish. This three-level scheme for making sense of culture – artifacts, or what is visible; espoused values, or what is said and proclaimed; and underlying assumptions and values, or what is truly felt and believed – comes from the influential organizational psychologist Edgar Schein, who studied the workplace cultures of modern businesses (2009). The first two levels derive from the third, which is mostly tacit and unarticulated. Culture, Schein argues, functions as a set of enduring and workable solutions to the problems of the group:

> Culture is a pattern of shared tacit assumptions that was learned by a group as
> it solved its problems of external adaptation and internal integration, that has
> worked well enough to be considered valid and, therefore, to be taught to new
> members as the correct way to perceive, think, and feel in relation to those
> problems. (Schein 2009, p. 27)

Schein's second level, espoused values, merits some scrutiny. "Espoused" is an
obscure word, often ignored by textbooks (for instance in organizational behavior, where the chapter on organizational culture always includes a mention of
Schein's three-level framework) and by students, who mistakenly focus only on
the accompanying word, "values." It is helpful to understand espoused values as
'claimed' values – those values that members of a group, especially those in
positions of authority, claim and proclaim as the group's true values. Espoused
values can be a cloak to conceal less positive values (greed, fear, aggression,
selfishness, for instance) that may inhere in the group's actual underlying
assumptions. The gap between espoused values and underlying assumptions
and values – I think of it as the B.S. gap – is a universal feature of modern
groups, especially business organizations.[9] But perhaps it is a feature of all
groups.

Culture serves as a set of stable answers to a group's five existential questions: 'Who are we?' 'Where are we?' 'Where are we going?' 'How do we get
there?' and 'What about me?' Over time, the answers, capturing ongoing
experiences and experiments, become remarkably rich and sophisticated:

> Botanists and naturalists have been continually amazed by the degree and
> breadth of knowledge hunters-gatherers have of the natural world around
> them. ... We might ... think of hunters and gatherers as having an entire
> library of almanacs: one for natural stands of cereals, subdivided into wheats,

---

[9] The years-long Wells Fargo scandal, which broke in 2016, is a well-known example of a big gap
between lofty claims and unethical actions. Wells Fargo was an old bank, founded in California in
the nineteenth century, that at the end of the twentieth century and the beginning of the twenty-
first grew rapidly, mainly through mergers that put new pressures on its identity. It published an
annual booklet, *The Vision & Values of Wells Fargo*, in 2015 credited to the authorship of its CEO,
John Stumpf. The booklet's pages proclaimed, "We value and support our team members as
a competitive advantage" ... "We value what's right for our customers in everything we do"
(Stumpf 2015, pp. 6, 9). At the same time, to keep the growth going, inside the company Stumpf
made "Eight is great!" his rallying cry – meaning that each customer should have, on average,
eight different accounts with the company, sold to them by energetic salespeople. For context, in
2019 the industry average, counting a customer's accounts not just with one bank but with
multiple institutions, was 5.3 (Payments Journal 2019). Middle managers, pushed by Stumpf
and other senior leaders, pressured salespeople to meet these impossible expectations, with the
result that millions of fraudulent bank accounts were opened in customers' names. It is worth
watching Sen. Elizabeth Warren's sharp questions and Stumpf's fumbling answers during his
appearance before the Senate Banking Committee in 2016 (www.youtube.com/watch?
v=xJhkX74D10M). For one perspective on what leaders might learn from the Wells Fargo
scandal, see Fox (2016).

barleys, and oats; one for forest nuts and fruits, subdivided into acorns, beechnuts, and various berries; one for fishing, subdivided by shellfish, eels, herring, and shad; and so on. What is perhaps just as astonishing is that this veritable encyclopedia of knowledge, including its historical depth of past experience, is preserved entirely in the collective memory and oral tradition of the band. (Scott 2017, pp. 89–90)

In recent decades there has been growing interest in traditional ecological knowledge, defined as "a cumulative body of knowledge, practice and belief, evolving by adaptive processes and handed down through generations by cultural transmission, about the relation of living beings (including humans) with one another and with their environment" (Berkes, Colding, and Folke 2000, p. 1252). Such knowledge, one scholar notes, "is born of long intimacy and attentiveness to a homeland and can arise wherever people are materially and spiritually integrated with their landscape" (Kimmerer 2002, pp. 432–33). Such a way of living is mostly vanished in the modern world, and when someone like the Muskogee poet (and former Poet Laureate) Joy Harjo wants to invoke it, she must sing an elegy: "Once we knew everything in this lush promise" (Harjo 2000, p. 19). The forgetting of indigenous knowledge is one of the great tragedies of modernity.

It is impossible to imagine a group (except a brand-new one, in its early days) without a culture. Two strangers marooned on an island would quickly begin to develop a culture in the form of daily experiments and explorations of their environment, shared assessments of what worked and what didn't, clashes and disputes, and, soon enough, emerging tacit agreement on how best to collaborate in order to survive and maintain vitality. Perhaps, though, with sufficient commitment to human suffering, culture can be extinguished. Primo Levi's 1947 book, *Se Questo È un Uomo* (*If This Is a Man*, published in English as *Survival in Auschwitz*), describes what he saw and experienced in Auschwitz: "a gigantic biological and social experiment" designed not simply to kill people but to destroy all human relationships. The brutal reduction of life in the camp leaves nothing but two groups, "the drowned" who have given up and quickly die, and "the saved," who desperately try to delay death by one scheme or another (Levi 1996, p. 97). Culture has been stamped out in the camp, Levi suggests, unless we take it as the cumulation of individual survival tactics filed away in the brains of those who saw and happened to survive. One of the lessons of Levi's book is that where there is no collaboration within a group (not including external collaboration with the oppressors), there is no culture. Indeed, then there is no group, just a collection of lost souls.

We should not idealize culture. It is not pristine – just about every culture imitates and appropriates from other cultures, adopting ideas that have worked elsewhere. Except as a matter of personal belief (which, to be sure, we feel deeply), one culture is not better or worse, or more authentic, than another – that is the relativist battle that Franz Boas waged and won in anthropology a century ago. Nor is culture a timeless magic box of solutions for human problems. Any given culture represents a set of solutions that worked at some period of time for some group in some competitive environment, and may still work – if things have not changed too much. When change does occur, especially if it is sudden or massive or ongoing, a group's culture may be an impediment to effective adaptation. Nor is culture consensual and harmonious. At every moment a group experiences roils of tension, opposition, and politics – perhaps small and latent, perhaps large and active – in the shaping and playing out of its culture. Subgroups and individuals fight to control or redefine the culture for their own benefit. The young and new entrants are always rising up with new or different ideas. Indeed the group's culture, looked at more closely, is a patchwork and tense interaction of little subcultures maintained by subgroups, marked by their own tacit boundaries and sometimes pushing against each other for more space. Such tensions are not signs of an imperfect or broken culture, but simply part of how culture works, as a field of contestation where people work out how to live together. People yoke their desires and identities to the group, but never fully.[10] Morally, there is no assurance that a culture's set of solutions will strike an observer as good or fair for every member of the group – quite the contrary, in fact, for embedded in every culture are biases, unequal allocations of costs and benefits, and injustices. Pointed outward, biases often incline the members of a group to distrust and disdain others, especially members of groups identified as past or present rivals or foes. Turned inward, often by a subgroup within the group, cultural biases may teach that some in the group are less valuable than others, not fully to be trusted, or not meriting a full measure of respect, voice, and agency.

Yet culture, considering all, remains an extraordinary and unique resource for enriching our lives and unlocking possibilities. It is a record of human survival rooted in experience and refined by imagination. It helps us remember and apply lessons. It is a stabilizing force, but it can change – at its own pace, which is to say slowly, unless a group is put under intense pressure. For almost all of our existence as a species culture has been the only way to provide us with stable answers to our questions about how to live and collaborate.

And then, with the invention of writing in the ancient Near East about six thousand years ago, a new way began to take shape.

---

[10] Except at the end of a dystopian novel like Orwell's *1984*: "But it was all right, everything was all right, the struggle was finished. He had won the victory over himself. He loved Big Brother" (Orwell 2021, p. 315).

Writing arose thousands of years after three great innovations: agriculture, the domestication of animals, and permanent settlements. People living in groups apparently were able to absorb these innovations without upending everything about how they lived and worked (Graeber and Wengrow 2021). But the invention of writing seems to mark a radical disjuncture. "Writing," the French anthropologist Claude Lévi-Strauss observed, "is a strange thing." He suggested it might

> be regarded as a form of artificial memory, whose development should be accompanied by a deeper knowledge of the past and, therefore, by a greater ability to organize the present and the future.... [Writing] made it possible to assemble workpeople by the thousand and set them tasks that taxed them to the limits of their strength. (Lévi-Strauss 1961 [1955], pp. 291–92)

Six decades later, synthesizing much subsequent research, the political scientist James Scott argued that the invention of writing was closely associated with the origin and rise of the state and its increased capacity to organize and exploit human labor. He notes that imaginative literature and all "the civilizational glories we associate with writing" only appeared centuries after writing's initial use "for bookkeeping purposes" (2017, p. 141). The earliest evidence of writing from Uruk (the city of Gilgamesh), he points out, is administrative: "lists, lists, and lists – mostly of grain, manpower, and taxes" (p. 142). The ability to maintain written records created new possibilities to manage labor and production. When writing was invented in Mesopotamia, and then independently in Egypt, China, and Mesoamerica, early states responded energetically:

> The entire exercise in early state formation is one of standardization and abstraction required to deal with units of labor, grain, land, and rations. Essential to that standardization is the very invention of a standard nomenclature, through writing, of all the essential categories—receipts, work orders, labor dues, and so on. The creation and imposition of a written code throughout the city-state replaced vernacular judgments and was itself a distance-demolishing technology that held sway throughout the small realm. Labor standards were developed for such tasks as ploughing, harrowing, or sowing. Something like "work points" were created, showing credits and debits in work assignments. Standards of classification and quality were specified for fish, oil, and textiles – which were differentiated by weight and mesh. Livestock, slaves, and laborers were classified by gender and age. In embryonic form, the vital statistics of an appropriating state aiming to extract as much value as possible from its land and people is already in evidence. (Scott 2017, p. 144)

Once writing is invented, we see the rapid rise of every element of what we mean by bureaucracy, helping give rise to early states. These early states were small and weak, and as Scott notes, "most of the world's population continued to live outside the immediate grasp of states and their taxes for a very long time," until about 1600 (p. 14). But the basic pattern of bureaucracy had appeared.

Bureaucracy is a mode of organizing work along putatively rational lines. It seeks to measure and classify everything. (Science as it has grown in the modern world – rational, rule-bound, and professionalized – is close kin to bureaucracy. Scientists are passionate, jealous, noble, ambitious, cautious, and politically attuned people, to be sure, but they are also among the world's most expertly trained bureaucrats.) Bureaucracy establishes rigid structures and offices. It assigns specific tasks to specific positions. It transforms people's natural and long-standing ability to creatively divide labor into an organizing principle that makes possible enormous hierarchies, layering bosses of individual work groups, supervisors over the bosses, and senior managers at the pinnacles of organization charts. Accompanying hierarchy and the formal division of labor are written rules governing how work is to be done, who reports to whom, and the kinds of expertise and training needed for particular positions. Through its workings bureaucracy generates an enormous amount of information, which it carefully records, preserves, and (in theory, at least) relies on to guide work. The 'document' becomes the key constitutive element of bureaucratic power, kept in 'files.' These troves of written rules, records, data, and analysis are a source of stability and power for the group. Access is controlled and often jealously restricted by those in position to do so. The sheer accumulation of written records eventually makes innovation, initiative, and change harder. A bureaucracy is in a sense a machine for gathering information about the world, processing that information, and using it to optimize its assigned tasks. The fact that the machine is built out of people is, from bureaucracy's perspective, incidental. The most influential twentieth-century effort to develop leadership principles for bureaucracy, Frederick Taylor's scientific management, tried to regularize the human element to make it as orderly and systematic as every other factor of production: "In the past the man has been first; in the future the system must be first" (Taylor 1998 [1911], p. iv).

The word 'bureaucracy' was invented in France in the eighteenth century, the era when it began to rapidly accelerate. It means, literally, 'rule by desks and offices.' Contrast this with democracy, 'rule by the people.' The impersonality of bureaucracy is a defining trait: left to its own logic, bureaucracy sucks the life out of human interactions in groups, and replaces it with impersonal, standardized processes and interactions. When workers are pressured in bureaucratic settings to put forth positive emotions, it can seem forced and artificial, and such emotional labor is a hidden kind of work (Hochschild 1983). Bureaucracy prefers a particular kind of writing: flat, empirical, impersonal, emotionless. One sign of bureaucracy's global triumph is that all young people today learn in school how to write in this mode. (Some of us get stuck in it: my little writing primer, *The Nuts and Bolts of College Writing*, teaches how to write in the official style but avoid its worst aspects, and even breathe life into it.)

The greatest scholar of bureaucracy, Max Weber, who lived about a century ago in the world's most advanced industrial power, Germany, explained why bureaucracy was emerging as the dominant force in human affairs:

> The decisive reason for the advance of bureaucratic organization has always been its purely *technical* superiority over any other form of organization. The fully developed bureaucratic apparatus compares with other organizations exactly as does the machine with the non-mechanical modes of production. Precision, speed, unambiguity, knowledge of the files, continuity, discretion, unity, strict subordination, reduction of friction and of material and personal costs – these are raised to the optimum point in the strictly bureaucratic administration. (Weber 1978, vol. 2, p. 973, emphasis in the original)

Weber is right: bureaucracy is technically superior to any other form of organization. If you want size, scale, complexity, and power – that is to say, if the solutions to the problems you face require those things – you need bureaucracy. If you want to feed eight billion people, you need well-developed bureaucracies able to support enormous global agricultural, food production, and food delivery systems. If you want to create and produce more than 11 billion vaccines at "warp speed," within a year, to end an epidemic, you need a bureaucracy (Government Accounting Office 2021; Richter 2021). If you want to land humans on the moon, or educate millions of children, or mass produce cars, or even just collect money from people to alleviate poverty or save a species, you need a bureaucracy.[11]

---

[11] Some may protest that these things need free markets alone to flourish. In theory, indeed, a 'free market' operates purely by means of voluntary exchange, supply and demand, and perfect information for buyers and sellers. But in practice, in the world as it exists and with people as they are, bureaucracy is necessarily intertwined with markets. First, because the elements of free markets (private property, contracts, and information) require governments to define and protect them, adjudicate disputes, and prevent market participants from damaging the market or imposing unacceptable harm on others. The resulting definitions and protections, enacted as laws and regulations and institutions to enforce them, undergird markets. Second, because companies themselves are bureaucratic institutions par excellence. Capitalism is a tension of disruptive creativity – the entrepreneurial function – and bureaucratic efficiency and order – the 'big business' function. That is one reason leadership in the modern world is hard, because business leaders are expected to be both bureaucratically skilled and constantly innovative. Many people don't recognize the bureaucracy that sustains capitalism because it is (mostly) radically decentralized, so that for instance there is not a "shipping bureaucracy," but a vast and nimble shipping industry, made up of thousands of small bureaucracies, mostly in the form of companies ceaselessly trying to outcompete each other with one innovation or another, applied as efficiently (i.e., bureaucratically) as possible.

And on and on: for instance, if you want to significantly improve health conditions in military hospitals, you need bureaucracy's comprehensive rationality. That's what 35-year-old Florence Nightingale soon realized in 1855, when she arrived at the British military hospital in Scutari (Shkodër in modern Albania) to oversee the care of wounded soldiers. Nightingale, born with a love of mathematics but not allowed to pursue her passion due to her culture's social mores about gender, found work superintending a care-house for sick women in London, and helping her friend Sidney Herbert, a Cabinet minister, survey hospitals about the working conditions of nurses. Herbert invited her to lead the first team of nurses sent to care for British soldiers wounded in the Crimean War. During her two years in the hospital in Scutari, it became increasingly urgent for her to figure out why so many soldiers were dying in the hospital. She relentlessly pursued answers, coming to realize that the system of health care was broken or absent. Her scrutiny of every detail, from floorplans to sunlight and fresh air to soap to vegetables, was extraordinary, as we see in a letter she wrote two months after arriving at the hospital:

> I am afraid to get back today to my immense first question, how this hospital is to be purveyed. . . . We ought to know (1) exactly how many beds there are in hospital, purveyed ready for use, (2) how many vacant, (3) how many patients to come in. Each ward ought to have its own complement of shirts, socks, bedding, utensils, etc., the new sick succeeding to the old sick's things – instead of keeping a caravanserai [inn], as we do; how the kitchen ought to be inspected; the washing ditto; clean shirts twice a week; instead of my cooking all the extra diets; getting all the vegetables thought necessary for scurvy. In fact, I am a kind of general dealer, in socks, shirts, knives and forks, wooden spoons, tin baths, tables and forms, cabbage and carrots, operating tables, towels and soap, small-tooth combs, precipitate for destroying lice, scissors, bedpans and stump pillows. (Nightingale 2002–12, vol. 14, pp. 104–5, brackets in the published text)

From this point on, Nightingale devoted her life to the statistical exploration of human health and well-being. She helped pioneer evidence-based health care. She sought not only to establish schools of nursing for young women, but to systematize how nursing was taught, to professionalize the career path of nurses, and broadly to subject every problem of poverty and public health in England to a systematic approach: data collection, statistical analysis, and rational reform underpinned by a driving moral commitment to help the poor. Nightingale became famous in England from her two years tending to the wounded of Crimea. Henry Wadsworth Longfellow, the American poet, immortalized her as the "Lady with a Lamp," as saintly (and as strangely passive, in his poem) as the Christian martyr Philomena. But she was no saint – she was a statistician who understood that big problems require big data. She grasped the power of telling stories with data, and was a pioneer in the visual display of quantitative information, devising a new kind of chart, her famous polar area diagram, to dramatize deaths caused by unsanitary conditions (Hedley 2020). Over the course of her life she refused to marry because, she wrote, it would distract from her work. She was impatient with adhering to gender expectations: "you want to do the thing that is good," she wrote in *Notes on Nursing*, "whether it is 'suitable for a woman' or not" (Nightingale 2002–12, vol. 6, p. 158). In 1860 she became the first woman elected to the Royal Statistical Society. She lived until she was 90 years, publishing more than 200 papers, reports, and books on hospitals, nursing, and public health. She did more than any other single person to professionalize the vocation of nursing, and helped establish the field of public health and the discipline of hospital epidemiology. In all of this, her life was a testament to the visionary application of bureaucracy to solve human problems. As the editor of her collected writings, Lynn McDonald, writes, "The need for accurate, relevant statistics went to the heart of Nightingale's mission" (Nightingale 2002–12, vol. 16, p. 560). Florence Nightingale's ability to lead with statistics suggests a path for contemporary leaders who must, one way or another, come to terms with bureaucracy.

But there is another side to bureaucracy. We have already glimpsed this in Primo Levi's description of Auschwitz. The idea to exterminate the Jews was conceived by a few truly evil individuals, and grew out of an old vein of anti-Semitism in Europe. But the implementation of the means to do so was inevitably bureaucratic, as detailed most famously in the fifteen-page *Protocol of the Wannsee Conference*, the working notes of the meeting of senior Nazi leaders held on January 20, 1942, in a Berlin suburb to formalize "the organisational, technical and material aspects of the final solution of the Jewish question" (*Protocol*, p. 2). The protocol specified the status of various categories of people, for instance, "first-degree *Mischlinge*," persons of mixed Jewish and non-Jewish parents or grandparents: "First-degree *Mischlinge* will be treated as Jews in regard to the final solution of the Jewish question" (p. 10).[12] Bureaucracy is a machine-like system for getting work done, especially work that can be standardized, scaled, and divided up. The machine can be used for good, or for evil.

---

[12] This category would have included the author of this Element. My great-great-aunt, Ida Wolle, née Rosenblatt, died, age seventy, in September 1942 at Theresienstadt, eight months after the *Protocol* delineated that camp's purpose: "The intention is not to evacuate Jews over the age of 65, but to transfer them to an old-people's ghetto – Theresienstadt has been earmarked for this purpose" (p. 8). This volume is dedicated to her.

Bureaucracy's mechanical attributes mean that it has little ability to directly provide answers to our deepest questions. It is of course very good at 'how.' But on the other 'we' questions ('who are we?' 'where are we?' 'where are we going?'), bureaucracy's greatest efficacy is to point us in the direction of empirical information. Very few organizations today would, for instance, change their mission, launch a bold new strategic direction, or reorganize their operations without extensive bureaucratic labor: analyzing their competitive situation, researching potential alternatives, modeling the outcomes of different possible choices. As for the individual emotional and moral energy that 'what about me?' bears, it would not seem that bureaucracy can help us much. And yet it provides tools to uncover and measure our feelings and fears and hopes, in the form of questionnaires, surveys, focus groups, records of behaviors and interactions and outcomes, all of which can be analyzed, summarized, and written up into reports to share with the organization at large, or at least managers or senior leaders. And it can provide a rational basis for appropriate, benchmarked compensation, job design, and professional development that create a framework for caring, if not caring itself. We have become so used to relying on bureaucratic modes for managing people and their interactions in groups that the only surprising thing about Pope Francis establishing a Human Resources Department in the Vatican in 2022 is that such an enormous old institution managed to go so long without one (Besmond de Senneville 2022).

"Bureaucracy must die," the noted business scholar Gary Hamel wrote in 2014. There is much to despair or loathe about its vision of "organizations without people," in the memorable phrase of Warren Bennis (1959, p. 263). Compared to our flesh-and-blood lives, quick brains, and flashing emotions, bureaucracy is slow, rigid, and uncaring. A culture has a rich emotional life; a bureaucracy is a vacuum of feelings. And little pockets of bureaucracies, loci of power, may be captured by special interests, which once entrenched become resistant to change. Like all machines, bureaucracy can break, and Weber's idealized portrait often falls short in the real world. But most of all, bureaucracy can create workplaces that are not only dehumanized, but anti-human. Henry Ford loved his factory – "The way to make automobiles is to make one automobile like another automobile, to make them all alike, to make them come through the factory just alike" (quoted in Chandler 1964, p. 28) – but listen to a worker in one of those car factories: "Repetition is such that if you were to think about the job itself, you'd slowly go out of your mind" (Terkel 1974, p. 221). Bureaucracy takes the group with its vibrant human life, social learning, and shared meaning making, and breaks it into pieces. It appoints managers to supervise, and teaches us to know our place in the org chart.

Many managers habituated to bureaucracy use questions not so much to spark creative thought as to stifle creativity and reinforce power dynamics: see Holmes and Chiles (2010) on questions as managerial "control devices." But leaders can push against this tendency. When the energetic Jack Welch became CEO of General Electric in 1981, he scrapped the time-honored tradition of using prepared binders of questions ("crib sheets filled with 'I gotcha' questions' ") in GE's annual planning reviews. In his memoir Welch explained:

> The last thing I wanted was a series of tough technical questions to score a few points. What was the purpose of being CEO if I couldn't ask my own questions? . . . For every business review, headquarters people loaded up their own staff heads with questions. We had dozens of people routinely going through what I considered "dead books." All my career, I never wanted to see a planning book before the person presented it. To me, the value of these sessions wasn't in the books. It was in the heads and hearts of the people who were coming into Fairfield. I wanted to drill down, to get beyond the binders and into the thinking that went into them. I needed to see the business leaders' body language and the passion they poured into their arguments. (Welch and Byrne 2001, pp. 93–94)

Sadly, Welch showed himself over the course of his twenty-year tenure as CEO to be the coldest bureaucrat of them all. He eroded GE's culture and human spirit with annual forced rankings and firings. He imposed an expectation that earnings reports must always beat expectations.[13] And he elevated dollars over every other measure of GE's value – a duly hard-edged capitalist, one might say, and widely lauded as an exemplar of business leadership, but see Gelles (2022) for a forceful critique of Welch and his legacy.

In this section we have looked at the two ways that groups can develop stable answers to their questions. Culture represents the shared wisdom of the group, built out of countless experiences and experiments. The knowledge it provides is deep and mostly tacit, and requires long immersion in the group to learn. Culture develops on the scale of the group, and links human experiences across years and even generations. It weaves past, present, and future into a living fabric of meaning and significance. Because it evolved with our species and we with it, culture's impact on us is strongly rooted and hard to extirpate. Bureaucracy, the

---

[13] James Martin, who worked at GE for six years in the 1980s, recalls in a memoir how, as a trainee fresh out of Wharton, he quickly learned how GE operated under Welch: "The first month I informed one executive that our results were coming in low, we probably weren't going to 'make our number.' . . . 'So what?' he said. 'Just reverse a few journal entries.' 'But that doesn't represent what we earned,' I said, full of four years of accounting beans. 'Listen,' he said implacably, 'each month we will put out a report and hit the right numbers or we'll get shit from Corporate. So just do whatever it takes to make those numbers' " (2000, pp. 33–34). Martin eventually left the corporate world to become a priest.

other way of providing stable answers for a group, is far more recent, and is more mechanical than human. It is weak in the ways culture is strong – connection to human identity and emotion, moral understanding, and sense of purpose. But it is immeasurably strong in its capacity to rationally organize work and scale it to unimaginable size and speed. As the life of Florence Nightingale shows, it can be a powerful tool in the hands of a passionate visionary. In our capitalist world culture grows weak and bureaucracy grows strong. Groups today, even companies, still develop cultures, but they are thin compared to the past. It is instructive, and amusing, to see how the owners of a company like Lululemon seek – quite effectively, one might note – to shape its culture as a piece of competitive advantage, even forbidding the mention of the past (Kowitt and Leahey 2013).

Perhaps bureaucracy itself is the emerging culture of modernity, slowly weaving itself into the fabric of every group, habituating us to be increasingly rational, efficient, punctual, empirical, uninterested in the past, eager for information delivered by devices, wary of the value of anecdote and lived experience, and less connected to the physical world and people directly around us. Strikingly, we are bureaucratizing childhood itself; children today have less freedom than in the past to play and explore the physical world (see Louv 2008 and Haidt 2024). But bureaucracy, when it dominates the life of a group, impels us to hold back a part of ourselves. The human spark eludes bureaucracy.

But it is the human spark that groups need, above all, when they face the crisis of disruptive change.

5 Disruptive Answers

> I kept stumbling and falling and stumbling and falling as I searched for the good. "Why?" I asked myself. Now I believe that I was on the right path all along, particularly with the Green Belt Movement, but then others told me that I shouldn't have a career, that I shouldn't raise my voice, that women are supposed to have a master. That I needed to be someone else. Finally I was able to see that if I had a contribution I wanted to make, I must do it, despite what others said. That I was OK the way I was. That it was all right to be strong.
>
> *Wangari Maathai (in Sears 1991, p. 55)*

The hills of Kenya were turning brown. The trees that had mantled them in green for longer than human memory were disappearing. Each day the women climbing the hills to find firewood had to go a little higher. Some wondered, "What will happen when there are no more trees?" Deforestation had been a problem in Kenya going back to the colonial era. In the 1940s, the British colonial government had addressed the problem through the *shamba* policy – allowing landless people whose lives had been disrupted by colonial seizure of traditional lands to clear public forests and plant them with trees like eucalyptus and cypress, commercially attractive timber that could be harvested and sold by the colonizers. Between the trees, people were allowed to plant subsistence crops, but as the trees grew they would have to find new land on which to survive. Before the coming of the colonizers, people had planted all kinds of trees – banana, mango, macadamia, moringo (whose root, bark, gum, leaf, fruit, flowers, seeds, and oil were all traditionally used as medicines for a range of ailments). The end of colonialism, when it came in 1963, didn't change much, as Kenyan politicians and their cronies now profited from selling timber and clearing forests for tea plantations. The trees were no longer for the people, and there were fewer and fewer of them.

Wangari Maathai, Kenya's great environmental activist, was born in 1940 in the central highlands to parents who worked on colonial plantations. She grew up in nature and loved the trees around her. Decades later, she recalled one great old fig tree that her mother told her was sacred and life-giving: "That tree inspired awe. It was protected. It was the place of God" (Hari 2009). She hated the colonial *shamba* system (Kanogo 2020, p. 75). After scoring high on national exams, she was one of several hundred east Africans (along with Barack Obama's father) offered college scholarships in the United States in the late 1950s and early 1960s. After studying in the United States and then in Germany, she came back to Kenya in the late 1960s to see, despite independence, that things were worse: "I went back to where I grew up, and I found God had been relocated to a little stone building called a church. The tree was no longer sacred. It had been cut down. I mourned for that tree" (Hari 2009).

In Kenya she earned a doctorate in 1971 and became a professor at the University of Nairobi, even becoming chair of her department (the first woman in east Africa to attain a doctorate and a chair). But eventually she lost her position, due in part to men's discomfort at a strong woman in such a role. It was a theme that would recur in her life. In 1969 she started a business to plant trees, but it failed. She started a nonprofit in 1976 to do the same thing; it also failed (pp. 71–72). Like Henry Ford, it took her three tries to get it right: in 1977 she started the grassroots Green Belt Movement, which took root and grew. Early on, progress was slow. "Nobody took us seriously at all," she recalled in 1989 about her early years as an activist. "Well, that is typical. First of all, we are women" (Hiltzik 1989). Maathai's idea was to involve rural people, especially women, in planting trees, and help people understand the deep connection between the life of trees and their own lives: "I always felt that our work was not simply about planting trees. It was about inspiring people to take charge of their environment, the system that governed them, their lives, and the future" (Green Belt Movement, n.d.).

In 1989 Maathai and the growing Green Belt Movement came into conflict with Kenya's dictatorial president, Daniel arap Moi, when he decided to build a sixty-story skyscraper in Nairobi's main green space, Uhuru Park. It was meant to be the commanding center of his political party and its extended activities, and included as a prominent part of its design a large statue of himself (Perlez 1989). Maathai, appalled by the loss of green space in the dense urban center of Kenya's capital, led protests against the planned building. The president called the Green Belt Movement "subversive," but international attention eventually compelled him to cancel the project (Gettleman 2011). In 1992, Maathai found her name on a list of activists targeted for assassination (Vidal 2011). That year, at a protest with the mothers of detained political prisoners, she was beaten unconscious by police (Neely 2009). A decade later, in her Nobel Peace Prize acceptance speech, Maathai reflected on how her effort to plant trees had grown to become a broader challenge to Kenya's settled order:

> Although initially the Green Belt Movement's tree planting activities did not address issues of democracy and peace, it soon became clear that responsible governance of the environment was impossible without democratic space. Therefore, the tree became a symbol for the democratic struggle in Kenya. . . . Through the Green Belt Movement, thousands of ordinary citizens were mobilized and empowered to take action and effect change. They learned to overcome fear and a sense of helplessness and moved to defend democratic rights. (Maathai 2004)

Maathai died of ovarian cancer in 2011, having inspired the planting of tens of millions of trees in Kenya and billions of trees around the world. As with many visionary leaders, she looked not only to the past, to traditional ways of living in close and sustainable connection with nature, but also, thanks in large part to her years in the United States ("America changed me in every way. I saw the civil rights movement. It changed what I knew about how to be a citizen, how to be a woman, how to live" (Hari 2009)), to a new world of equal rights and fuller lives for women in Kenya and beyond. Today, her vision is mostly unrealized, and in Kenya deforestation continues. But her work still influences others, including a global campaign to combat climate change by planting one trillion trees (St. George 2022). And her words still have the power to inspire: "I am a daughter of the soil, and trees have been my life" (Hari 2009).

When groups face pressing problems, especially when these are new or newly urgent, then culture and bureaucracy – meant to provide stability and incremental change – struggle to provide useful answers. It is in such times that an unknown individual like Wangari Maathai can come forward with just a question or an idea. Often the disruptive spark starts with something small, like planting a tree or helping a small group of new believers find a safe place to worship. But it may be that the effort to implement the idea reveals another problem standing in the way, and then another, and eventually a whole fabric begins to come apart, and needs to be woven anew. The disruption that a leader brings may not be widely perceived or understood, at first, but it is there in the first spark.

Bold disruptions often provoke fierce resistance from within the group. Mohandas Gandhi, for instance, perceived from a distance as an almost miraculously successful transformational leader who peacefully brought British colonial rule in India to an end, faced often intense opposition within India. Gandhi came from a wealthy and politically powerful family. He traveled and studied abroad, worked as a lawyer in South Africa, and gained close familiarity with Western and other cultural traditions of philosophy and religion. He was a devout Hindu, but he refused to be limited by the authority of tradition, instead developing his own broad humanistic understanding – he was, for instance, greatly influenced by Tolstoy's Christian pacifism. He signaled his independence of thought by titling his memoir (2018, originally published serially between 1925 and 1929) *Experiments in Truth*. His unique synthesis of beliefs and his willingness to focus on his primary goal, a unified and free India, brought him into conflict with many in India. B. R. Ambedkar, the great political leader of low-caste Indians, disdained Gandhi for his unwillingness to do more to challenge the injustice of caste. Muhammed Jinnah, leader of India's Muslims, rejected Gandhi's vision of a common Indian identity above different faiths, and pushed for the security of Muslims by partition and the establishment of Pakistan. But it was a fanatical member of a third group, ethno-nationalist Hindus, who assassinated Gandhi in 1948. The assassin, Nathuram Vinayak Godse, believed that Gandhi had betrayed India's Hindu identity by enabling partition and accommodating other groups. Remarkably, as Hindu nationalism has risen to power in India, Godse has become increasingly popular. Across India more than a dozen statues of Gandhi's assassin have been put up in recent years, and in some Hindu temples he is worshipped. One Hindu nationalist explains the veneration of Godse: "It is because of Gandhi and his ideology that India was divided and Hindus had to bow before Muslims and outsiders" (quoted in Andrabi 2023). Another put it more brutally: "Gandhi was a traitor. He deserved to be shot in the head" (quoted in Yasir 2020).[14]

There is no guarantee that an envisioned disruption will ever come into being. Sometimes all that happens is that a question gets asked. The disruptive question may not even be new. It may have been asked generation after

---

[14] On Gandhi's life and legacy, see Ramachandra Guha's two-volume biography (2014 and 2018) and his history of India after Guha (2019). On Gandhi's conception and use of nonviolent power, see Dalton (2012).

generation, waiting for an answer. Frederick Douglass in 1852: "What, to the American slave, is your 4th of July?" (1996, p. 118). W. E. B. DuBois in 1897: "Between me and the other world there is ever an unasked question ... How does it feel to be a problem?" (2007, p. 7). Gwendolyn Brooks in 1973: "Are there ways, is there *any* way, to make English words speak blackly?" (Brooks 1973, p. xxix, emphasis in the original). In November 1963 Malcolm X made the question of identity for his audience – black activists attending the Northern Negro Grass Roots Leadership Conference at King Solomon Baptist Church in Detroit – the crux of his searing "Message to the Grass Roots." The speech, especially its arresting opening, is an intricately contrived symphony of plain speaking meant to bring its listeners to a revolutionary conclusion:

> We want to have just an off-the-cuff chat between you and me – us. We want to talk right down to earth in a language that everybody here can easily understand. We all agree tonight, all of the speakers have agreed, that America has a very serious problem. Not only does America have a very serious problem, but our people have a very serious problem. America's problem is us. We're her problem. The only reason she has a problem is she doesn't want us here. And every time you look at yourself, be you black, brown, red, or yellow – a so-called Negro – you represent a person who poses such a serious problem for America because you're not wanted. Once you face this as a fact, then you can start plotting a course that will make you appear intelligent, instead of unintelligent.

The rhetoric is striking in its simplicity: plain diction, "facing facts," the invoking of the ordinary desire to appear intelligent. Next, a call for unity that dismisses America's common categories of difference and reduces identity to a single brutal binary:

> What you and I need to do is learn to forget our differences. When we come together, we don't come together as Baptists or Methodists. You don't catch hell 'cause you're a Baptist, and you don't catch hell 'cause you're a Methodist. You don't catch hell 'cause you're a Methodist or Baptist. You don't catch hell because you're a Democrat or a Republican. You don't catch hell because you're a Mason or an Elk. And you sure don't catch hell 'cause you're an American; 'cause if you was an American, you wouldn't catch no hell. You catch hell 'cause you're a black man. You catch hell, all of us catch hell, for the same reason.

Malcolm X now uses his simple style to shatter the simple American founding myth:

> So we are all black people, so-called Negroes, second-class citizens, ex-slaves. You are nothing but a ex-slave. You don't like to be told that. But what else are you? You are ex-slaves. You didn't come here on the

Mayflower. You came here on a slave ship – in chains, like a horse, or a cow, or a chicken. And you were brought here by the people who came here on the Mayflower. You were brought here by the so-called Pilgrims, or Founding Fathers. They were the ones who brought you here.

Malcolm X concludes his extraordinary exordium with a bleak and radical answer to the question of identity: "We have a common enemy. . . . But once we all realize that we have a common enemy, then we unite – on the basis of what we have in common" (X 1965, pp. 4–5, but transcribed as spoken, according to the audio recording).[15]

Malcolm X's ability to elicit strong emotional reaction to his words was extraordinary. According to the theologian James H. Cone, "Martin Luther King once said that when he listened to Malcolm speak, even he got angry" (quoted in Blake 2010). King, of course, had his own, sharply different understanding of black identity as "deeply rooted in the American dream" – drawing inspiration from, and woven into, the promises, the espoused values, the uncashed "check" written out in America's founding, as King envisioned in his own immortal 1963 speech (King 1986, pp. 217, 219).

Six decades on from the great era of civil rights legislation and King and Malcolm X (and four centuries since whites initiated the enslavement of blacks in America), it is fair to say that something historically meaningful has been achieved to shape a new, widely accepted American identity more inclusive of all its citizens, and truer to the nation's espoused founding values. It took tumult and the patient toil of many. It may even be that Malcolm X's stark accusing answer to the question of 'who are we?' helped bring about the sea-change. Laws – bureaucracy – can be altered at the stroke of a pen.[16] But to change the deep-seated foundational beliefs of a culture is the work of generations. Frederick Douglass, whose speech in 1852 – perhaps the greatest speech in American history (see Colaiaco 2006) – was as searing and accusatory as Malcolm's, nevertheless ended it with soaring, poetic imagery that calls forth the vast transforming possibilities of time and space:

The far off and almost fabulous Pacific rolls in grandeur at our feet. The Celestial Empire, the mystery of ages, is being solved. The fiat of the

---

[15] Ralph Ellison used the same radicalization of identity in *Invisible Man* (1952), in the last words of the protagonist's grandfather: " 'Son, after I'm gone I want you to keep up the good fight. I never told you, but our life is a war and I have been a traitor all my born days, a spy in the enemy's country ever since I give up my gun back in the Reconstruction. . . . Learn it to the younguns,' he whispered fiercely; then he died" (Ellison 1952, pp. 13–14).

[16] As hard won, and as consequential, as that stroke may be. Nick Kotz's *Judgment Days* (2005) tells the extraordinary story of how Martin Luther King, Jr. and President Lyndon Johnson forged an uneasy collaboration to win passage of two historic civil rights laws: the Civil Rights Act of 1964 and the Voting Rights Act of 1965.

> Almighty, *'Let there be Light,'* has not yet spent its force. (Douglass 1996,
> p. 129, emphasis in the original)

Leadership's deepest working – its capacity to transform people in their hearts –
is mysterious (see Burns 1978 and 2003).

In popular imagination a single figure can swiftly bring extraordinary change.
The charismatic leader speaks and a kingdom falls, or begins to rise. But
charismatic authority – a real and important phenomenon, and a significant
element of leadership (Riggio 2006) – is complex, unstable, and fragile. The
demand for it increases in times of distress, as people lose confidence in their
accustomed cultural and bureaucratic institutions. In response, an individual
may offer themself as a bearer of solutions, arrived at not by rational analysis or
adherence to tradition, but by an explicit rejection of these, and recourse instead
to an unexplained inner creative process that hints of the magical or divine. But
charisma does not only appear in times of crisis. The offering of charismatic
authority is actually a common part of our lives. The scholar Charles Lindholm
observes that scholars have tended to ignore "its role in daily life," noting that
"charismatic figures continue to appear as political/religious leaders or anti-
establishment rebels in highly developed nation-states" (2021, p. 47). Every day
we encounter aspirants for charismatic leadership, offering us a glimpse of their
answers to the problems that afflict us, promising special access to secret
knowledge if we choose to accept their authority. Most of the time, such aspiring
charismatics are unheard or ignored, or attract only a small community of
followers among those who have become disenchanted with the circumstances
of their lives. Max Weber, as part of his lifelong study of human collaboration,
explored charisma as incisively as bureaucracy. He sharply contrasts charismatic authority, sudden and new, with the ponderous gathered mass of bureaucratic authority:

> In radical contrast to bureaucratic organization, charisma knows no formal
> and regulated appointment or dismissal, no career, advancement or salary, no
> supervisory or appeals body, no local or purely technical jurisdiction, and no
> permanent institutions in the manner of bureaucratic agencies. . . . Charisma
> is self-determined and sets its own limits. Its bearer seizes the task for which
> he is destined and demands that others obey and follow him by virtue of his
> mission. If those to whom he feels sent do not recognize him, his claim
> collapses; if they recognize it, he is their master as long as he "proves"
> himself. . . .
>   Charismatic authority is naturally unstable. The holder may lose his
> charisma, he may feel "forsaken by his God," as Jesus did on the cross . . . ;
> it may appear to his followers that "his powers have left him." Then his
> mission comes to an end, and hope expects and searches for a new bearer; his
> followers abandon him, for pure charisma does not recognize any legitimacy

other than one which flows from personal strength proven time and again.
(Weber 1978, vol. 2, pp. 1112–14)

"Charismatic domination," Weber wrote, "transforms all values and breaks all traditional and rational norms" (p. 1115). The true charismatic leader develops an inner group of true believers "adapted to the mission of the leader. The personal staff constitutes a charismatic aristocracy composed of a select group of adherents who are united by discipleship and loyalty and chosen according to personal charismatic qualification" (p. 1119).[17] Weber concluded that charisma as a mode of authority, a human response to crisis in the life of a group, can only exist for a limited period of time: "Every charisma is on the road from a turbulently emotional life that knows no economic rationality to a slow death by suffocation under the weight of material interests: every hour of its existence brings it nearer to this end" (p. 1120).

The leader as disruptor is part of the mythology – but also the real practice – of business. Within companies, these disruptions are often felt as attacks upon a company's culture or bureaucracy, or both. That is not surprising, because culture, bureaucracy, and leadership are the only three ways that groups have for finding answers to their questions, and they are always in tension. Jack Welch was conscious of this tension at the start of his tenure at GE, and sought out opportunities to challenge entrenched bureaucracy and long-established culture: "In those days, I was throwing hand grenades, trying to blow up traditions and rituals that I felt held us back" (Welch and Byrne 2001, p. 97). In his first year he was invited to speak to the annual leadership conference of the company's elite social club, Elfun. Instead of what most new CEOs would do (celebrate GE's history, praise the traditions of Elfun, confess humility, and express confidence in the future if they worked together), he used the occasion to challenge Elfun itself, while he looked out at the audience of GE veterans gaping up at him: " 'I can't find any value to what you're doing. You're a hierarchical social and political club. I'm not going to tell you what you should do or be. It's your job to figure out a role that makes sense for you and GE.' " He recalled the impact: "There was stunned silence when I finished the speech." A month later, he relates in his memoir, Elfun began to shift to a new identity and mission, organizing community volunteering by GE employees around the world. "Elfun's self-engineered turnaround," Welch says, "became a very important symbol. It was just what I was looking for" (Welch and Byrne 2001, p. 98). Another CEO, Bob Iger, shows the same willingness to challenge

---

[17] See Eric Hoffer's *The True Believer* (1951) for a classic study, as well as Lindholm (1990), especially the chapters on Adolf Hitler and the Nazi party and on Jim Jones and the Peoples Temple.

culture, even at as venerable and storied a company as Disney: "You can't allow tradition to get in the way of innovation. There's a need to respect the past, but it's a mistake to revere your past" (Ignatius 2011).

Sometimes the disruption is more comical. When the CEO of BetterUp, a struggling career coaching startup, wanted to use a Zoom staff meeting to announce a new strategy and shake the company up, he donned a train conductor's cap and blew a whistle each time he announced a change. "It was one of the most awkward calls I've ever been on professionally," recalled an employee (Kirsch 2023). Elon Musk, two weeks after buying Twitter and one week after mass layoffs, summoned the remaining workers to their first meeting, and tried to establish his own dynamic energy as a new work mode:

> Okay, collectively, you'll do it. Great. Please do it. Let's take action. I'm a big believer in having just a maniacal sense of urgency. So if you can do it after this meeting, I would do it after this meeting. Just a maniacal sense of urgency. Like, if you want to get stuff done, maniacal sense of urgency. Just go "aah!" Hardcore! (Heath 2022)

Musk has followed up his initial disruptions with many more. His success in disrupting X (the company formerly known as Twitter) into profitability is an ongoing experiment.

Many business disruptions consist of a new answer to the 'how' question, in the form of a structural reorganization. This was the spark of the Alfred Sloan story at General Motors. When Sloan took charge in 1923, he reformed GM from a shapeless collection of car companies often competing with each other ('cannibalizing sales,' in the striking term of art) into its enduring divisional structure, which became a model for countless other corporations facing the challenge of balancing vast size and operational agility.[18] Sloan led General Motors for more than three decades. His memoir, published in 1964 and still read by students of business, shows the liveliness of his thinking, his patient and empathetic handling of individuals, and his humanistic grasp of the need for leaders to be both masters of precise detail and askers of big questions. He ends his book (1990, p. 444) with a stirring evocation of the rhythm of change and creativity:

> Each new generation must meet changes – in the automotive market, in the general administration of the enterprise, and in the involvement of the corporation in a changing world. For the present management, the work is

---

[18] In 2015, for instance, Google's founders, Larry Page and Sergey Brin, did the same thing for the same reasons, reshaping their increasingly sprawling company into a divisionalized entity, Alphabet: see Page's (2015) admirably lucid memorandum to employees, "G is for Google."

only beginning. Some of their problems are similar to those I met in my time; some are problems I never dreamed of. The work of creating goes on.

A number of popular books have explored the power of questions in business and other work settings. Michael Marquardt argues that asking questions can allow leaders "to let go of their ego-driven need to have their own answers. They drop their need to be right, and so they can allow others to be right" (2005, p. 172). Dov Seidman (2007) and Simon Sinek (2009) encourage an interrogative spirit – Seidman stressing 'how' and Sinek 'why' – as helping to shape effective, resilient, and human-centered work environments. Warren Berger explores the power of the "beautiful question" – "an ambitious yet actionable question that can begin to shift the way we perceive or think about something" (2014, p. 8) – to spark creative thinking and change. Jeffrey Liker's *The Toyota Way* (2004) details how Toyota became the world's most admired and imitated manufacturing company. Toyota's senior leaders, far more than leaders of American companies, have long sought to integrate the company's formal operational structure, its culture, and its leadership into a set of practices that emphasize learning and thoughtful innovation throughout the company. Central to Toyota's culture, Liker argues, is a spirit of inquiry, visible for instance in the famous "five-why" method: Toyota trains workers and managers, when they grapple with problems of all kinds – for instance, an oil spill on a shop floor, a problem frequently used in Toyota's training – to ask 'why' five times, each time digging deeper, trying to uncover the root cause of the problem (Liker 2004, p. 135). Other important inquiry-oriented concepts at Toyota include *hansei* (reflection) and *genchi genbutsu* (literally, "actual place, actual thing"), best translated in Toyota's culture as "go and see for yourself" – a core teaching for managers to get out of their offices and see the real, physical place, and the human–machine interactions, where a problem is occurring or a process might be improved. Peter Senge, in his subtle best-selling study of how organizations learn, *The Fifth Discipline: The Art & Practice of the Learning Organization* (1990), cautions that inquiry alone may end up as a barrier to true learning: "just asking lots of questions can be a way of avoiding learning – by hiding our own view behind a wall of incessant questioning" (p. 199). Senge (following the noted scholar Chris Argyris: see for instance Argyris 1999) instead recommends "reciprocal inquiry," a deliberate linking of asking questions and revealing one's own answers or beliefs: "By this we mean that everyone makes his or her thinking explicit and subject to public examination" (p. 199). True reciprocal inquiry is hard to sustain, as there are often powerful social motivations for concealing or at least softening one's thoughts and questions in a group. Like all social practices, inquiry can become performative and political.

Pat Summitt, one of the greatest coaches in college basketball (her teams at the University of Tennessee won eight NCAA Division I championships), relied on a framework of questions to help shape her coaching. For instance, reflecting on the start of the season for one of her championship teams – the 1997–98 team, full of new players – she writes, "we would start with something as simple and fundamental as our names. We had to decide who we were. Every team has its own personality and character. We needed to get to know ours" (Summitt and Jenkins 1998a, p. 20). In another book she writes about the challenge of forging a true team out of a collection of self-regarding individuals: "I request, I plead, I threaten. . . . I talk about teamwork until I have no voice left. But when I'm done with my speech, some of them still look at me skeptically, as if to say, 'Yeah, but what's in it for me?' " (Summitt and Jenkins 1998b, p. 162). "Teamwork," Summitt concludes, "is a highly tenuous state" (p. 162), requiring constant work to build trust, align goals, manage moods and egos, and notice and solve problems. Summitt's leadership reflections are worthy of study because of her deep practical wisdom, honed over four decades of coaching – but also because she had to constantly guard against the more destructive aspects of her own fiery and controlling nature. Following a diagnosis of early-onset Alzheimer's disease, Summitt retired from coaching at age fifty-nine. She died four years later. Her last book (Summitt and Jenkins 2013) is a poignant self-portrait of a driven and competitive leader, used throughout her life to winning everything she sets her mind to, suddenly confronting her mortality.

Sometimes groups develop ways to control the power of questions to disrupt. The catechism, examples of which are common in many branches and orders in Western Christianity, consists of a list of questions that might occur to a thoughtful person encountering the teachings of the religion – but with official answers to be memorized and repeated. The word derives from a Greek word meaning 'oral instruction.' A catechism replicates the format of asking and answering, but without the essence of inquiry, the freedom to think for yourself. From the perspective of a group with established values and beliefs, shaping the beliefs and understandings of group members is an important function. But it is startling to contemplate, especially from the perspective of the individual. Every restraint on the space to ask questions and explore answers, even if it stabilizes a group, does so by weakening the individual's free inquiry. One of the most striking examples of subordinating individual understanding to the strictures of the group comes from St. Ignatius, the sixteenth-century Spanish saint who founded the Society of Jesus. The Jesuits are famous among Christian orders for their fearless commitment to critical inquiry, education, and impact in the world, yet St. Ignatius, in his *Spiritual Exercises* (1548), wrote, "What I see as white, I will believe to be black if the hierarchical Church thus determines it" (Ignatius of Loyola 1991, p. 213).

Let us close this section by considering the engineer, statistician, and management consultant W. Edwards Deming, once famed as the father of what was called Total Quality Management. The particular managerial systems that Deming helped develop have, over time, tended to harden into bureaucratic and somewhat lifeless modes of organizing work (Lean Manufacturing or Six Sigma, for instance), and the spark of purpose that Deming sought to breathe into our understanding of work flickers, at best. It is hard to maintain a constant human spark in the face of relentless bureaucracy, pitiless economic competition, and the cold realities of work in dynamic, contract-based entities. But Deming had no doubts that he was hewing enduring practical wisdom, and even philosophy, out of the daily experiences of people working. (He is deeply honored in Japan, where he helped rebuild the national industrial fabric after the devastation of the Second World War.) Deming, like Florence Nightingale, believed in the power of statistics and statistical analysis to solve human problems. And, like her, he understood in a profound way that organizations tasked with work are not only bureaucracies and assemblies of productive power, but also human communities, and that any investigation of "work" must mean attention to the nature, the thoughts, the feelings, the aspirations, and the questions of the human beings who do the work. Deming's most famous book is *Out of the Crisis* (1982). Among its eighteen chapters, dense with facts and reflections on industrial processes, productivity, and statistical process control (as well as many thoughtful stories and musings), Deming devotes one chapter (Chapter 5, "Questions to Help Managers") to a long list of questions (2000 [1982], pp. 156–66).[19] The questions are precise and technical ("How do you select foremen?" "How much incoming material turns out to be totally unusable in the judgment of the production managers?"), but none of them are simply narrow: all of them encourage reflection about how to do things well, keeping in mind that one is working with people as well as machines and systems. From Deming's first question ("Has your company established constancy of purpose?"), continuing through surprising ones to read from a statistician ("Are you guilty of setting numerical goals on the factory floor for production?"), to questions that point to deeper areas of meaning and purpose ("Do you encourage self-improvement of your people? How? In what way?" "Do you run your company on visible figures alone?" "What is your company doing for the community?"), the chapter showers upon the reader

---

[19] For a more recent collation of questions for managers and aspiring leaders, see chapter 3, "Asking Artful Questions," in Donna Ladkin's *Mastering the Ethical Dimension of Organizations* (2015).

a cascade of 214 questions, without any interpolated text, that go far beyond narrow instrumental concerns about how to wring more efficiency and profit from work.

Deming never forgot the human beings who do the work – nor the active effort at practical philosophy that wise leaders should engage in, every day, not only to disrupt but also to sustain their groups and understand the reality of their situation, and the reality they are trying to enact. The question he poses most often in his mighty chapter of interrogatories is a simple one: "How do you know?"

6 What about Us?

> Everyone has a slice of genius. Your role as a leader is to unleash their genius and harness it for the collective good.
>
> *Linda A. Hill (2023)*

Leaders, through their questions and answers, disrupt groups. But just as important as disruption is the renewing of stability. Through the flux of challenge and change, effective collaboration must soon emerge if the group is to hold together and get anything done. Thus a leader must be not only a disruptor but also a weaver. Perhaps the greatest ongoing source of disruption to a group is not any one person's questions or ideas but us ourselves, in our infinite variety of identities and understandings and interests. Weaving together people in their diversity is an old way of understanding leadership, expressed for instance in Plato's *Statesman*, which conceives the leader's chief task as weaving "different kinds of people into one political fabric" (quoting the editors of a modern (1995) edition, p. xii). Sometimes the impulse to weave a single fabric goes so far as to try to suppress any deviation of thought (Plato again, with his fantastical elaboration of the "noble lie" in the *Republic* (1991), 414d-415d, pp. 93–94). But it is more common to be satisfied with what John Gardner (1990) termed "workable unity" (p. 16). That is what I take to be the American understanding of its old motto, *E pluribus unum* ("out of many, one"): not an *unum*, a one, of perfect identity, but a boisterous, many-voiced community, with disagreements and different ideas as sharp and deep as the beliefs that unite.[20]

Another tension that leaders must grapple with is the tension of time. The members of a group live in the present, each busy with their work, and judged according to whether they have met this or that deadline. For its part, bureaucracy focuses the group's work on the time spans that it can most easily access

---

[20] Walt Whitman, the poet of American democracy, said it best in *Leaves of Grass*: "Do I contradict myself? / Very well then I contradict myself. / (I am large, I contain multitudes)" (2001, p. 113).

and exert control over: the recent past, the present, and the near future, analyzed in neat and regular time increments. Culture looks farther back into the past, and if it looks to the future at all it is with anxiety, or a hope for restoration. Only leadership, by its very nature, peers into the unknown future and works to shape it into reality.[21] For some CEOs and similar bosses this leads to frustration: "Why doesn't anyone here care as much as I do about the challenges and risks racing toward us?" They forget that while they are judged and rewarded on their ability to navigate the group into the future, others are punished if they stray too far from the present, and the work at hand. So leaders must be able to set one foot in the future and one in the present, and bridge the gap.

Often they do so by invoking the past. Lincoln's extraordinary Gettysburg Address, delivered in the middle of a civil war, is perhaps the best example of a leader weaving together, in just three neat paragraphs and an astonishingly concise 272 words, the past ("Fourscore and seven years ago," the speech's biblically resonant opening words), the present ("Now we are engaged in a great civil war," the word "Now" marking the start of the second paragraph), and the future: "we here highly resolve that these dead shall not have died in vain – that this this nation, under God, shall have a new birth of freedom – and that government of the people, by the people, for the people, shall not perish from the earth" (Lincoln 1953, vol. 7, p. 24). Rarely has so vast a vision been evoked in so few words.

Collins and Porras' *Built to Last* (1994) argues that the most successful companies learn how to weave together disruption and stability. Despite sailing in the sea of change, they manage to hold on to an enduring identity, founded on "pragmatic idealism" (p. 48) that is about more than maximizing profits, and that conveys to employees a meaningful, even moral understanding of their shared work. At the same time, Collins and Porras say, such companies embrace audacious reinvention ("BHAGs," or "big hairy audacious goals," p. 93). Ron Heifetz's *Leadership without Easy Answers* (also published in 1994) makes a similar argument about the necessary weaving together of "technical" work, which optimizes the existing routines, habits, and capacities of the group, and "adaptive" work, which helps a group and its people learn how to change.

More recently Harvard Business School professor Amy C. Edmondson has argued that some leaders fail because they "were simply thinking about their roles in the wrong way. They thought they needed to provide answers, when instead they needed to ask the right questions" (2012, p. 4). Edmondson argues

---

[21] The venerable managerial technique SWOT (Strengths-Weaknesses-Opportunities-Threats) analysis, while often poorly taught or understood (see Minsky and Aron 2021), is a useful forward-looking tool that encourages open exploration of a group's competitive situation and possible futures.

that successful organizations escape the trap of thinking of leadership as a one-person function, and embrace its collaborative nature: "When leaders empower, rather than control; when they ask the right questions, rather than provide the right answers; and when they focus on flexibility, rather than insist on adherence, they move to a higher form of execution" (p. 8). Similarly, another Harvard Business School professor, ethnographer Linda Hill, describes in an interview how she helps companies develop a question-centered approach:

> we looked at a leader at Proctor and Gamble and one of the things they did is they literally have coaches come and coach the C-suite executives on how many statements they made versus how many questions they asked. And they ended up deciding there were four questions they should always ask. What have you learned? How did you learn it? What else do you need to learn? How can I help? (in Ignatius 2022)

Sometimes, though, a leader feels that the questions are so dangerous, or the answers so unsettling, that they suppress them. In 1946, around the same time that Sister Mary Teresa Bojaxhiu, on a train in India, heard the voice of God calling her to devote her life to the poor, she began to lose her faith. For the rest of her life, even as she founded religious orders, attracted tens of thousands of women and men to take vows and join her, and became a global icon of the power of faith, "darkness," as she called it, enveloped Mother Teresa. Throughout her life she had suffered bouts of depression. But from now on, for fifty years (with one brief respite of a few weeks), she lived an interior life of darkness, feeling only spiritual desolation:

> Where is my faith? – even deep down, right in, there is nothing but emptiness & darkness . . . – I have no faith. – I dare not utter the words & thoughts that crowd in my heart – & make me suffer untold agony. So many unanswered questions live within me – I am afraid to uncover them. . . . (Teresa 2007, p. 187)

Teresa hid it all inside: "The whole time smiling. – Sisters & people . . . think my faith, trust & love are filling my very being & that the intimacy with God and union to His will must be absorbing my heart. – Could they but know" (p. 187). For years she begged her confessors and other church confidantes to destroy the letters she had sent them, worried that they would shake others' faith and damage her work. When her doubts were eventually published, some indeed struggled to reconcile her agonized life with their faith in her faith. One of these was Mary Johnson, for twenty years a sister in Teresa's order, the Missionaries of Christ. As a teenager Johnson was inspired by the Teresa story to devote her life to service in Christ. She took her first vows at about the same age as the young Teresa (then Gonxha Bojaxhiu) had done a half-century earlier. But eventually Sister Donata (Mary's new name in Teresa's order) began to question her own faith. After two decades she left the order. In her memoir she relates learning, a decade after she had left the church, about Teresa's life in the darkness. She was angry at the church for hiding Teresa's true feelings and pushing her to interpret the darkness as her way to be close to God. And she felt sad for Teresa, and how she dealt with her life of doubting: "Mother's questions gave way to a dogmatic decision to believe. She would avoid future doubts by uncompromising insistence on Church teaching" (Johnson 2012, p. 517). And she wondered about the impact on others who trusted Teresa. A life of service to the poor was good and meaningful – but the chasm between Teresa's inner doubts and her public life of faith, meant to continue to attract new adherents to her orders, troubled her:

> So many people throughout the world have been moved by the stories of a perfect Mother, a holy Mother who loves each person, and who always smiled, even when she didn't feel like it. I feel odd to prefer the human to the perfect; maybe that's part of why I don't fit anymore. I want earth, not heaven. (p. 521)

When leaders move us to upend and even risk our lives, what do we really know about their real thoughts and motivations? Shakespeare puts this question at the heart of *Henry V.* The play has often been understood as a full-throated celebration of England's charismatic young warrior king, who won a glorious victory over the French at Agincourt. Shakespeare employs a Chorus as a kind of stand-in for those among the common people who love their king; the Chorus paints a rousing picture of Henry's charisma, bravery, and faith. But against this, Shakespeare persistently undermines the simple belief that Henry's war is just. The actual Henry is calculating, strategic, and always working to manage situations and people's understanding of those situations. Others are also revealed as intensely political. In the play's opening scene, the Archbishop of Canterbury – who in the next scene will give the war its religious stamp of approval – tells a confidant that he's going to support the war to forestall a new tax on the church. The play's deepest moment is an unexpected dialogue, the night before the battle of Agincourt, between a disguised king and an ordinary soldier, Williams. Not realizing he's talking to the king, Williams tells Henry that he doubts the soldiers can trust their king to fight with them to the end. Henry says that they can take comfort from the King's "cause being just and his quarrel honourable." "That's more than we know," Williams answers acerbically (Shakespeare 1969, p. 764, 4.1.119–22). He delivers a vivid indictment:

> if the cause be not good, the King himself hath a heavy reckoning to make, when all those legs and arms and heads chopped off in a battle shall join together at the latter day, and cry all, "We died at such a place"—some

swearing, some crying for a surgeon, some upon their wives left poor behind
them, some upon the debts they owe, some upon their children rawly left.

"I am afeard," Williams concludes with stunning force, "there are few die
well that die in a battle; for how can they charitably dispose of anything,
when blood is their argument?" (4.1.128–37). In a play that on its most
accessible level celebrates the bravery and faith of a charismatic king,
Shakespeare gives a common soldier the courage and wisdom to ask, in
effect, 'What about us?'

Well, what about us? This Element has argued that leadership is not a property
of a few people with special talent or status. There is a spark of leadership in each
of us. It is our innate drive to ask, and to use our answers as a foundation for
meaningful action in the world. In that regard, at least, it is akin to Nietzsche's
conception of the inborn will to power (Williams 1996). But unlike Nietzsche's
idea, the spark of leadership knows no gender, and connects rather than divides
us. It is embedded in our DNA and expressed in our natural ability to breathe life
into even the bleakest shared experience. If you have read Arthur Koestler's novel
Darkness at Noon (1941), think of Rubashov and the other prison inmates, kept in
solitary confinement and politically at odds, yet talking by tapping on the thick
stone walls. Call it the will to share meaning. I tend to think it arose by blind
chance and stuck around because it proved adaptive for our species. But perhaps it
is a touch of the divine. We all have a spark of leadership, and thus of connection
to people and the world, even if we busy ourselves in solitary, shut-up spaces.
Everyone sometimes looks up at the stars and wonders. "Fresh courage," says the
poet Joy Harjo, "glimmers from the planets" (2000, p. 20).

However others may perceive you, however you may fear that your inner
truth falls short, remember this: you carry, by virtue of your humanity, a spark of
leadership. It is a precious gift. But it is also a responsibility. To embrace our full

Figure 1 The group's five existential questions

humanity we must tend our spark and use it to contribute to something larger than ourself, a community that needs our help. Our unsocial sociability may make it hard, but it will also help us keep trying. Nurturing your spark of leadership doesn't mean you need to contend for the leader's role. But it does mean you should cultivate your own phronesis, your practical wisdom. Be mindful and curious. Observe and wonder. Ask, and encourage others' questions. And if a would-be, so-called "leader" steps forth to bully, mock, or bludgeon others into silence, understand that that is not the way of the leader, however furious the insistence that black is white and lies are truth.

Share your spark of leadership with humility – but with pride in your plain and precious humanness. And if you do choose to lead, even for just a moment or just one question, you may perceive that you have begun to live a life that feels somehow fuller and richer. Like the legendary Gilgamesh and the barely glimpsed Lydia and the copiously documented Florence Nightingale and the fearless Wangari Maathai, and countless others who dared to ask, you did something to help a group endure, and to help people live better and truer lives.

The problems we face will remain with us. We'll keep asking questions about how to understand and solve them. New and baffling problems will arise, and require new thinking. The work of creating, as Alfred Sloan said, goes on. But at the heart of it all, as old as our species, are five simple questions we have always asked and always will: 'Who are we?' 'Where are we?' 'Where are we going?' 'How do we get there?' 'What about me?' The asking and the answering is nothing more, and nothing less, than the human condition.

The circle turns, and groups come and go. In each group we, or people like us, kindle a light of meaning in the world. Perhaps the world is waiting for us to make the light bright enough to see everything – including all the ways we are connected to each other, and to the world itself.

What do you think?

And what might you do about it?

Coda: Lincoln and Lee

The crux of the Civil War was a moral question: 'Who is a human being?' The words and actions of the two major Civil War leaders – President Abraham Lincoln and General Robert E. Lee – show how, at a critical moment, each one wrestled with and answered the great question of their time.

Abraham Lincoln in 1860

> Whether we will it or not, the question of Slavery is the question, the all absorbing topic of the day. . . . Whenever this question shall be settled, it must be settled on some philosophical basis. No policy that does not rest upon some philosophical public opinion can be permanently maintained.
>
> *Abraham Lincoln, speech at New Haven, Connecticut,*
> *March 6, 1860 (Lincoln 1953, vol. 4, p. 27)*

As 1860 began, fifty-year-old Abraham Lincoln aspired to be president. The moral issue of slavery, he believed, had reached a crisis point and could no longer be extemporized or evaded. Slavery would either spread and destroy the promise of the United States, or be extinguished. Decades of compromise had only worsened America's political tensions. In the 1850s the North was emerging as demographically and economically dominant, but the South responded by becoming more aggressive in legislation (the Kansas-Nebraska Act of 1854) and judicial opinion (the Supreme Court's *Dred Scott* decision of 1857). By the end of the 1850s one of the two old political parties, the Whigs, had died. The other, the Democrats, had broken into two factions: north and south. A new Republican Party opposed to slavery had recently arisen. To complete the roster a cobbled-together Constitutional Union party was attempting to forge an alliance of unionist moderates in the north and south. Lincoln's understanding of the crisis was rooted in a moral vision of the evil of slavery. But it was shaped by his awareness of the complex dynamics of American politics in 1860, and by his deeply political nature.[22] He sought to frame his bold agenda for change – a clear path to the extinction of slavery – as nothing more than continuity with the past, rather than innovation. The road to freedom, in his artful telling, was a fulfillment of America's founding ideals and a continuation of the new nation's first laws. He was not alone in this effort to seize the past: southerners were making a similar effort to entrench enslavement as a central element of the nation's founding and identity. Indeed, they had been increasingly successful,

---

[22] William Herndon, Lincoln's lifelong friend and law partner, left a memorable description: "That man who thinks Lincoln calmly sat down and gathered his robes about him, waiting for the people to call him, has a very erroneous knowledge of Lincoln. He was always calculating, and always planning ahead. His ambition was a little engine that knew no rest" (Herndon and Weik 1889, vol. 1, p. 375).

most recently with the *Dred Scott* decision (1857) that wrote black people out of the Constitution. Thus the great political battle of the era was not simply between two different moral visions, but two different claims about the meaning and aspirations of American democracy, and the links between past and present as they might shape the future.

At the start of 1860 Lincoln was a battle-scarred veteran of Illinois politics little known outside his home state. He had been politically active for almost thirty years, losing elections about as often as he won them. He had served in, and lost races for, the Illinois state legislature and the U.S. House of Representatives. Twice he had failed to win election to the U.S. Senate, in 1854 and 1858. When his old political party, the Whigs, faded into irrelevance, he joined the new Republican Party in 1856. After gaining some recognition among Republicans in his failed 1858 Senate bid, his strategy in 1860 was to make himself known to eastern Republicans, win the party nomination at the convention in his backyard, Chicago, and, in a divided electorate, maximize turnout among his supporters to obtain a winning share of electoral votes. He thus eagerly accepted an invitation from New York Republicans to speak in New York City early in 1860. It was an opportunity to build his brand in the northeast, and he spent countless hours researching and planning his talk. On February 27, two weeks after his 51st birthday, he delivered his Cooper Union address. In it he made an eloquent argument, composed as carefully as a lawyer's brief, that the Founding Fathers had opposed slavery, and had taken actions to limit its spread and encourage its eventual extinction. When Lincoln spoke the next day in Providence, Rhode Island, even the editor of a Democratic paper called it "the finest constitutional argument for a popular audience that I ever heard" (Burlingame 2008, vol. 1, p. 591). In New Haven, Connecticut, a week later, Lincoln argued that his position was truly the conservative one, not new and radical, as southerners charged:

> What is conservatism? Is it not adherence to the old and tried, against the new and untried? We stick to, contend for, the identical old policy on the point in controversy which was adopted by our fathers who framed the Government under which we live; while you with one accord reject, and scout, and spit upon that old policy, and insist upon substituting something new. ... Not one of all your various plans can show a precedent or an advocate in the century within which our Government originated. And yet you draw yourselves up and say "We are eminently conservative!" [Great laughter.] (Lincoln 1953, vol. 4, p. 27)

"By the time his Eastern tour ended," a biographer says, "Lincoln had achieved a new status and attracted a horde of political supporters" (Burlingame 2008, vol. 1, p. 591).

The Republican convention was held in Chicago in May in a specially built wooden structure called the Wigwam, stuffed with 465 delegates and 10,000 spectators and partisans, many of them, thanks to counterfeit tickets and forged signatures orchestrated by Lincoln's men, loyal Lincoln supporters. Lincoln's strategy was to be a popular second choice among the state delegations, ready to emerge if the leading candidate, William Seward, fell short on the first ballot. Lincoln's team worked his public image (the frontier-friendly "Rail Splitter" and plain-speaking "Honest Abe") and rough-edged tactics, including neutralizing a hostile Illinois newspaper editor and politician: "Lincoln operatives had a critic follow him in his wake denouncing him" (p. 608). Lincoln's strategy worked, and he won the nomination on the third ballot (Achorn 2023). The subsequent presidential campaign was hard-fought, but on Tuesday, November 6, 1860, Abraham Lincoln was elected the 16th president of the United States. In the fragmented political environment, he was elected by voters in the North and the West. Virtually no votes were cast for him in the fifteen Southern slave states. Nationally, Lincoln won just under 40 percent of the total vote. But it sufficed.

Robert E. Lee in 1861

> The great question which is now uprooting this Government to its foundation – the great question which underlies all our deliberations here, is the question of African slavery.
>
> *Thomas F. Goode, speech to the Virginia Secession Convention,*
> *March 28, 1861 (Reese 1965, vol. 2, p. 518)*

After Abraham Lincoln's election in November 1860, many Southern whites felt that the pillars of their civilization – white supremacy and black enslavement – were in peril. On December 20, South Carolina seceded from the Union. Six states soon followed, and the Confederate States of America declared their existence on February 8. On March 21, Alexander Stephens, the Confederacy's Vice President, delivered his astonishing "Cornerstone" speech asserting the fundamental idea of the secession:

> The prevailing ideas entertained by [Jefferson] and most of the leading statesmen at the time of the formation of the old constitution, were that the enslavement of the African was in violation of the laws of nature; that it was wrong in principle, socially, morally, and politically. It was an evil they knew not well how to deal with, but the general opinion of the men of that day was that, somehow or other in the order of Providence, the institution would be evanescent and pass away. ... Those ideas, however, were fundamentally wrong. ... Our new government is founded upon exactly the opposite idea; its foundations are laid, its corner-stone rests, upon the great truth that the negro

> is not equal to the white man; that slavery – subordination to the superior race – is his natural and normal condition. . . . This, our new government, is the first, in the history of the world, based upon this great physical, philosophical, and moral truth. (Stephens 2008, p. 61)[23]

Yet the state of Virginia wavered. Two weeks after Stephens' speech, delegates to Virginia's secession convention voted almost two-to-one against secession. But a week later, on April 12, after Abraham Lincoln had refused to abandon Fort Sumter in South Carolina, Confederate forces attacked it. The Civil War had begun. President Lincoln called on the states to raise federal troops, and a storm of protest swept the south. On April 17, in a second vote at the Virginia convention, delegates voted 88–55 to secede.

Robert E. Lee now faced the great moral choice of his life: loyalty to his nation or to his state. He himself opposed secession. But he was an owner of enslaved people. His family's wealth and status depended on enslavement. And his heart was with the white people of Virginia. Three days after Virginia's vote to secede, he resigned his commission in the United States Army. That day he wrote to his sister in Maryland:

> Now we are in a state of war which will yield to nothing. The whole South is in a state of revolution, into which Virginia, after a long struggle, has been drawn; and though I recognise no necessity for this state of things, and would have forborne and pleaded to the end for redress of grievances, real or supposed, yet in my own person I had to meet the question whether I should take part against my native State.
>
> With all my devotion to the Union and the feeling of loyalty and duty of an American citizen, I have not been able to make up my mind to raise my hand against my relatives, my children, my home. I have therefore resigned my commission in the Army, and save in defense of my native State, with the sincere hope that my poor services may never be needed, I hope I may never be called on to draw my sword. I know you will blame me; but you must think as kindly of me as you can, and believe that I have endeavoured to do what I thought right. (Lee 2019, p. 14)

Lee came from a prominent plantation family in Virginia. Two of his ancestors signed the Declaration of Independence. His father was Henry Lee III, "Light Horse Harry," a hero of the American Revolution and a governor of Virginia. His wife was a great-granddaughter of Martha Washington. From the perspective of traditional white Southern culture, Lee is a hero, a great leader, a courtly and inspirational figure who wrestled with his conscience and chose, in the end, to be true to his heritage, stay with his people, and fight a doomed battle.

---

[23] On Stephens and his speech, see Hebert (2021).

But it is more accurate to say that Lee failed his most crucial leadership test. Rather than helping white Virginians see truth and end evil, rather than challenging people to think in new ways and grow morally as Abraham Lincoln would give his life to achieve, Lee turned inward, avoided hard questions, and invoked a mythic past as his vision of the future. Notably, other Virginians in the western part of the state (not so rich, not so celebrated, not so financially dependent on slavery) rejected the secession vote and stayed loyal to the Union. Two of Lee's own Virginia cousins – Samuel Phillips Lee and John Fitzgerald Lee – kept their commissions and served the Union throughout the Civil War. Samuel, who became a Rear Admiral in the U.S. Navy, is credited with a memorable quip: "When I find the word Virginia in my commission, I will join the Confederacy" (Hoehling 1993, p. 6). Indeed, of nine colonels from Virginia in the U.S. Army in 1861, Lee was the only one to resign his commission (National Park Service, n.d.).

Lee's precious Virginia was not helped by his choice to join the Confederacy. Indeed, his personal example and seeming virtues contributed to the myth of the south and the "lost cause." Lee's choice helped entrench and legitimize white supremacy long after the war, and left a legacy of hatred, violence, and injustice masked as patriotic reverence that still does harm in Virginia, the south, and America today. Even if, somehow, Lee had won, he would in truth have lost. To the great "question of African slavery" that his fellow Virginian Thomas Goode posed at the secession convention, Robert E. Lee's answer, stamped in blood, was yes, and forever.

Bibliography

Achebe, Chinua. 1974 [1964]. *Arrow of God*. New York: Anchor Books.

1989 [1966]. *A Man of the People*. New York: Anchor Books.

1994 [1958]. *Things Fall Apart*. New York: Anchor Books.

Achorn, Edward. 2023. *The Lincoln Miracle: Inside the Republican Convention That Changed History*. New York: Grove Atlantic.

Alicke, Mark D. Alicke and Olesya Govorun. 2005. "The Better-Than-Average Effect." In Mark D. Alicke, David A. Dunning, and Joachim I. Krueger, eds., *The Self in Social Judgment*. New York: Psychology Press, pp. 85–106.

Amman, Wolfgang and Jenson Goh, eds. 2017. *Phronesis in Business Schools: Reflections on Teaching and Learning*. Charlotte, NC: Information Age.

Andrabi, Jalees. 2023. "Gandhi's Killer a Hero to India's Diehard Hindu Nationalists." *New Straits Times* (January 27). www.nst.com.my/opinion/columnists/2023/01/874036/gandhis-killer-hero-indias-diehard-hindu-nationalists.

Argyris, Chris. 1999. *On Organizational Learning*, 2nd ed. Oxford: Blackwell.

Aristotle. 2002. *Nicomachean Ethics*, trans. Joe Sachs. Newburyport, MA: Focus Publishing.

2011. *Nicomachean Ethics*, trans. Robert C. Bartlett and Susan D. Collins. Chicago: University of Chicago Press.

Arnold, Jeanne E., Scott Sunell, Benjamin T. Nigra et al. 2016. "Entrenched Disbelief: Complex Hunter-Gatherers and the Case for Inclusive Cultural Evolutionary Thinking." *Journal of Archaeological Method and Theory* 23 (June), pp. 448–499.

Ascough, Richard S. 2009. *Lydia: Paul's Cosmopolitan Hostess*. Collegeville, MN: Liturgical Press.

Ashford, Susan and James R. Detert. 2015. "Get the Boss to Buy In: Learn to Sell Your Ideas Up the Chain of Command." *Harvard Business Review* 93:1–2 (January-February), pp. 72–79.

Atalay, Enghin. 2022. *A Twenty-First Century of Solitude? Time Alone and Together in the United States*. WP 22–11. Philadelphia: Federal Reserve Bank.

Augustine. 1986. *Concerning the City of God Against the Pagans*, trans. Henry Bettenson. New York: Penguin.

Austin, Robert D. and Gary P. Pisano. 2017. "Neurodiversity as a Competitive Advantage." *Harvard Business Review* 95:3 (May–June), pp. 96–103.

Avolio, Bruce J. and William L. Gardner. 2005. "Authentic Leadership Development: Getting to the Root of Positive Forms of Leadership." *The Leadership Quarterly* 16:3 (June), pp. 315–338.

Badger, Jonathan N. 2013. *Sophocles and the Politics of Tragedy: Cities and Transcendence*. New York: Routledge.

Barnett, George A. and Meihua Lee. 2002. "Issues in Intercultural Communication Research." In W. B. Gudykunst and B. Mody, eds., *Handbook of International and Intercultural Communication*, 2nd ed. Thousand Oaks: Sage.

Bell, Madison Smartt. 2007. *Toussaint Louverture: A Biography*. New York: Pantheon Books.

Bennis, Warren G. 1959. "Leadership Theory and Administrative Behavior: The Problem of Authority." *Administrative Science Quarterly* 4:3 (December), pp. 259–301.

Berger, Warren. 2014. *A More Beautiful Question: The Power of Inquiry to Spark Breakthrough Ideas*. New York: Bloomsbury.

Berkes, Fikret, Johan Colding, and Carl Folke. 2000. "Rediscovery of Traditional Ecological Knowledge as Adaptive Management." *Ecological Applications* 10:5, pp. 1251–1262.

Besmond de Senneville, Loup. 2022. "Pope Francis Appoints Vatican's First-ever HR Director." *La Croix International* (September 6). https://international.la-croix.com/news/religion/pope-francis-appoints-vaticans-first-ever-hr-director/16552.

Blake, John. 2010. "Malcolm and Martin, Closer Than We Ever Thought." CNN (May 19). www.cnn.com/2010/LIVING/05/19/Malcolmx.king/index.html.

Boesche, Roger. 2003. "Kautilya's Arthasastra on War and Diplomacy in Ancient India." *The Journal of Military History* 67:1 (January), pp. 9–37.

Boroujerdi, Mehrzad, ed. 2013. *Mirror for the Muslim Prince: Islam and the Theory of Statecraft*. Syracuse: Syracuse University Press.

Buchanan, Allen and Russell Powell. 2015. "The Limits of Evolutionary Explanations of Morality and Their Implications for Moral Progress." *Ethics* 126:1 (October), pp. 37–67.

Brooks, Gwendolyn. 1973. Introduction to *The Poetry of Black America: Anthology of the 20th Century*, ed. Arnold Adoff. New York: HarperCollins, pp. xxix–xxxi.

Burlingame, Michael. 2008. *Abraham Lincoln: A Life*. 2 vols. Baltimore: Johns Hopkins University Press.

Burns, James MacGregor. 1978. *Leadership*. New York: Harper & Row.

2003. *Transforming Leadership: A New Pursuit of Happiness*. New York: Grove Press.

Cain, Susan. 2012. *Quiet: The Power of Introverts in a World That Can't Stop Talking*. New York: Crown.

Carlyle, Thomas. 2013. *On Heroes, Hero-Worship, and the Heroic in History*. Eds. David R. Sorensen and Brent E. Kinser. New Haven: Yale University Press.

Carroll, Maurice. 1985. "Cuomo, at Yale, Urges Democrats to Remain with Tested Principles." *New York Times* (February 16), pp. 1, 26.

Chandler, Alfred D. Jr., ed. 1964. *Giant Enterprise: Ford, General Motors, and the Automobile Industry*. New York: Harcourt, Brace, & World.

Ciulla, Joanne B., ed. 2014. *Ethics, the Heart of Leadership*, 3rd ed. Santa Barbara, CA: Praeger, 2014.

Colaiaco, James A. 2006. *Frederick Douglass and the Fourth of July*. New York: St. Martin's Griffin.

Collins, James C. and Jerry I. Porras. 1994. *Built to Last: Successful Habits of Visionary Companies*. New York: HarperCollins.

Conger, Jay A., Rabindra N. Kanungo, and Sanjay T. Menon. 2000. "Charismatic Leadership and Follower Effects." *Journal of Organizational Behavior* 21:7 (November), pp. 747–767.

Cosans, Christopher E. and Christopher S. Reina. 2018. "The Leadership Ethics of Machiavelli's *Prince*." *Business Ethics Quarterly* 28:3 (July), pp. 275–300.

Crenshaw, James L. 1992. "Book of Job." In *The Anchor Bible Dictionary*, ed. Noel Freedman. 3 vols. New York: Doubleday, pp. 858–868.

Dalton, Dennis. 2012. *Mahatma Gandhi: Nonviolent Power in Action*. New York: Columbia University Press.

David, Richard H. 2015. *The Bhagavad Gita: A Biography*. Princeton: Princeton University Press.

De Angelis, Luigi, Francesco Baglivo, Guglielmo Arzilli et al. 2023. "ChatGPT and the Rise of Large Language Models: The New AI-driven Infodemic Threat in Public Health." *Front Public Health* 11 (April). https://doi.org/10.3389/fpubh.2023.1166120.

Dekmejian, R. Hrair and Adel Fathy Thabit. 2000. "Machiavelli's Arab Precursor: Ibn Ẓafar al-Ṣiqillī." *British Journal of Middle Eastern Studies* 27:2 (November), pp. 125–137.

Deming. W. Edwards. 2000 [1982]. *Out of the Crisis*. Cambridge, MA: MIT Press.

Dess, Gregory, Gerry McNamara, Alan Eisner, and Steve Sauerwald. 2024. *Strategic Management: Text and Cases, 11th Edition*. New York: McGraw Hill.

Dikötter, Frank. 2019. *How to Be a Dictator: The Cult of Personality in the Twentieth Century*. New York: Bloomsbury.

Douglas, Will. 2023. "The Inside Story of How ChatGPT Was Built from the People who Made It." *MIT Technology Review* (March 3). www.technolo gyreview.com/2023/03/03/1069311/inside-story-oral-history-how-chatgpt-built-openai/.

Douglass, Frederick. 1996. *The Oxford Frederick Douglass Reader*, ed. William L. Andrews. New York and Oxford: Oxford University Press.

Drucker, Peter F. 2003. *A Functioning Society: Selections from Sixty-five Years of Writing on Community, Society, and Polity.* New York: Transaction Press.

2004. "'What Needs to Be Done,' Peter Drucker on Leadership." Interview with Rich Karlgaard. *Forbes* (November 19). https://www.forbes.com/2004/11/19/cz_rk_1119drucker.html?sh=7e9755126f48.

Drucker, Peter F. Jim Collins, Philip Kotler et al. 2008. *The Five Most Important Questions You Will Ever Ask About Your Organization.* San Francisco: Jossey-Bass.

DuBois, W. E. B. 2007. *The Souls of Black Folk*, ed. Brent Hayes Edwards. Oxford World's Classics. New York: Oxford University Press.

Edmondson, Amy C. 2012. *Teaming: How Organizations Learn, Innovate, and Compete in the Knowledge Economy.* San Francisco: Jossey-Bass.

2018. *The Fearless Organization: Creating Psychological Safety in the Workplace for Learning, Innovation, and Growth.* New York: Wiley.

Ellison, Ralph. 1952. *Invisible Man.* New York: Random House.

Etieyibo, Edwin and Polycarp Ikuenobe, eds. 2020. *Menkiti on Community and Becoming a Person.* Lanham, MD: Rowman & Littlefield.

Farber, David. 2002. *Sloan Rules: Alfred P. Sloan and the Triumph of General Motors.* Chicago: University of Chicago Press.

Fayol, Henri. 1987 [1916]. *General and Industrial Management*, revised by Irwin Gray. New York: Pittman.

Fellows, Richard G. and Alistair C. Stewart. 2018. "Euodia, Syntyche and the Role of Syzygos: Phil 4:2–3." *Zeitschrift für die neutestamentliche Wissenschaft* 109:2, pp. 222–234.

Ferry, David, trans. 1992. *Gilgamesh: A New Rendering in English Verse.* New York: Farrar, Straus, and Giroux, 1992.

Fitzsimmons, Terrance W. and Victor J. Callan. 2020. "The Diversity Gap in Leadership: What Are We Missing in Current Theorizing?" *The Leadership Quarterly* 31:4 (August), pp. 103–147.

Fox, Tom. 2016. "Ethics Corner: Wells Fargo: The Lessons of an Ethics Failure." *National Defense* 101:757 (November–December), p. 10.

François, Gélineau, François, J. Daniel Montalvo and Valerie Schweizer-Robinson, eds., 2021. *Political Culture of Democracy in Haiti and in the Americas 2021: Taking the Pulse of Democracy.* Nashville: LAPOP.

Frank, Andrew. N.d. "Creek Indian Leaders." *New Georgia Encyclopedia.* Georgia Humanities and Athens: University of Georgia Press. www.geor giaencyclopedia.org/articles/history-archaeology/creek-indian-leaders/.

Fry, Louis W. 2003. "Toward a Theory of Spiritual Leadership." *The Leadership Quarterly* 14:6 (December), 693–727.

Fuentes, Agustín. 2017. *The Creative Spark: How Imagination Made Humans Exceptional.* New York: Dutton.

Gabel, John B. and Charles B. Wheeler. 1990. *The Bible as Literature: An Introduction,* 2nd ed. New York: Oxford University Press.

Galbraith, John Kenneth. 1977. *The Age of Uncertainty.* Boston: Houghton Mifflin.

Gandhi, Mohandas. 2018. *An Autobiography or The Story of My Experiments with Truth: A Critical Edition,* trans. Mahadev Desai. New Haven: Yale University Press

Gardner, John W. 1990. *On Leadership.* New York: Free Press.

Garfield, Zachary H. ; Christopher von Rueden ; and Edward H. Hagen. 2019. "The Evolutionary Anthropology of Political Leadership." *The Leadership Quarterly* 30:1 (February), pp. 59–80.

Gelles, David. 2022. *The Man Who Broke Capitalism: How Jack Welch Gutted the Heartland and Crushed the Soul of Corporate America – and How to Undo His Legacy.* New York: Simon & Schuster.

George, Bill. 2003. *Authentic Leadership: Rediscovering the Secrets to Creating Lasting Value.* San Francisco, CA: Jossey-Bass.

Gettleman, Jeffrey. 2011. "Wangari Maathai, Peace Prize Laureate, Dies at 71." *New York Times* (September 27), p. A25.

Goethals, George R. and Crystal L. Hoyt, eds. 2017. *Women and Leadership: History, Theories, and Case Studies.* Great Barrington, MA: Berkshire.

Goffman, Erving. 1961. *Asylums: Essays on the Social Situation of Mental Patients and Other Inmates.* Garden City: Anchor Books.

Goleman, Daniel, Richard Boyatzis, and Annie McKee. 2004. *Primal Leadership: Unleashing the Power of Emotional Intelligence.* Boston: Harvard Business School Press.

Gosling, Jonathan. 2013. "Things Fall Apart: Chinua Achebe." In Jonathan Gosling and Peter Villiers, eds, *Fictional Leaders: Heroes, Villains, and Absent Friends.* London: Palgrave Macmillan, pp. 99–112.

Government Accounting Office. 2021. *Operation Warp Speed: Accelerated COVID-19 Vaccine Development Status and Efforts to Address Manufacturing Challenges.* GAO-21–319. Washington, DC: Government Accounting Office (February 11). www.gao.gov/products/gao-21–319.

Graeber, David and David Wengrow. 2021. *The Dawn of Everything: A New History of Humanity.* New York: Farrar, Straus, and Giroux.

Green Belt Movement. N.d. "The Nobel Peace Prize." www.greenbeltmove ment.org/wangari-maathai/the-nobel-peace-prize.

Guha, Ramachandra. 2014. *Gandhi Before India*. New York: Knopf.

2018. *Gandhi: The Years That Changed the World, 1914–1948*. New York: Knopf.

2019. *India After Gandhi: The History of the World's Largest Democracy*, rev. ed. New York: HarperCollins.

Gutmann, Martin. 2023. *The Unseen Leader: How History Can Help Us Rethink Leadership*. New York: Springer.

Haidt, Jonathan. 2024. *The Anxious Generation: How the Great Rewiring of Childhood Caused an Epidemic of Mental Illness*. New York: Penguin Press.

Hamel, Gary. 2014. "Bureaucracy Must Die." *Harvard Business Review* (November 4). https://hbr.org/2014/11/bureaucracy-must-die/.

Hamilton, Alexander, James Madison, and John Jay. 1961. *The Federalist Papers*, ed. Clinton Rossiter. New York: New American Library.

Hare, Brian and Vanessa Woods. 2020. "Survival of the Friendliest." *Scientific American* 323:2 (August), pp. 58–63. www.scientificamerican.com/art icle/humans-evolved-to-be-friendly/.

Hari, Johann. 2009. "The Savior of Africa – and the Environment? An Interview with Nobel Prize-winner Wangari Maathai." Huffington Post (September 27). www.huffpost.com/entry/the-saviour-of-africa-a_b_301353.

Harjo, Joy. 2000. *A Map to the Next World: Poetry and Tales*. New York: W. W. Norton.

Hartmann, Hauke and Peter Thiery. 2022. *Global Findings BTI 2022*. Gütersloh, Germany: Bertelsmann Stiftung.

Harvey, Michael. 2008. "Against the Heroic: Gilgamesh and His City." In *Leadership and the Humanities*, volume 3 of *Leadership at the Crossroads*, general editor Joanne B. Ciulla. Westport, CT: Praeger Press, pp. 51–65.

2011. "Questioning Leadership: An Integrative Model." In *Leadership Studies: The Dialogue of Disciplines*, eds. Michael Harvey and Ronald E. Riggio. Cheltenham: Edward Elgar, pp. 199–229.

2020. *The Nuts and Bolts of College Writing*, 3rd ed. Indianapolis: Hackett.

ed. 2022. *Dead Precedents: Donald Trump in Historical Perspective*. London: Routledge/Taylor & Francis.

Harvey, Michael and Ronald Riggio, eds. 2011. *Leadership Studies: The Dialogue of Disciplines*. Cheltenham: Edward Elgar.

Haslam, S. Alexander, Stephen D. Reicher, and Michael J. Platow. 2020. *The New Psychology of Leadership: Identity, Influence and Power*, 2nd ed. New York: Routledge.

Heath, Alex. 2022. "Inside Elon Musk's First Meeting with Twitter Employees." *The Verge* (Nov. 10). theverge.com/2022/11/10/23452196/elon-musk-twitter-employee-meeting-q-and-a.

Hebert, Keith. 2021. *Cornerstone of the Confederacy: Alexander Stephens and the Speech that Defined the Lost Cause.* Knoxville: University of Tennessee Press.

Hedley, Alison. 2020. "Florence Nightingale and Victorian Data Visualisation." *Significance* 17:2 (April, Special issue: Florence Nightingale), pp. 26–30.

Heifetz, Ronald A. 1994. *Leadership without Easy Answers.* Cambridge: Harvard University Press.

Heifetz, Ronald A. and Donald L. Laurie. 1997. "The Work of Leadership." *Harvard Business Review* 75:1 (January), pp. 124–134.

Herndon, William H. and Jessie W. Weik. 1889. *Herndon's Lincoln: The True Story of a Great Life.* 3 vols. Chicago: Belford, Clarke.

Hewlett, Sylvia Ann ; Carolyn Buck Luce, and Cornel West. 2005. "Leadership in Your Midst: Tapping the Hidden Strengths of Minority Executives." *Harvard Business Review* 83:(11) (November), pp. 74–82.

Hill, Linda A. 2023. Keynote address. AACSB International Conference and Annual Meeting (Chicago, April 24).

Hiltzik, Michael A. 1989. "Skyscraper Prompts an Environmental Uproar." *Los Angeles Times* (December 17). www.latimes.com/archives/la-xpm-1989-12-17-mn-1678-story.html.

Hinchliffe, Emma. 2023. "Women CEOs Run 10.4% of Fortune 500 Companies." *Fortune* (June 5). https://fortune.com/2023/06/05/fortune-500-companies-2023-women-10-percent/.

Hochschild, Arlie Russell. 1983. *The Managed Heart: Commercialization of Human Feeling.* Berkeley: University of California Press.

Hoehling, Adolph A. 1993. *Thunder at Hampton Road.* Cambridge, MA: Da Capo Press.

Hoffer, Eric. 1951. *The True Believer: Thoughts on the Nature of Mass Movements.* New York: Harper & Row.

Holmes, Janet and Tina Chiles. 2010. "'Is That Right?' Questions and Questioning as Control Devices in the Workplace." Ch. 9 of Alice Freed and Susan Ehrlich, eds., *Why Do You Ask? The Function of Questions in Institutional Discourse.* New York: Oxford University Press, pp. 187–210.

House, Robert J. 1977. "A 1976 Theory of Charismatic Leadership." In J. G. Hunt & L. L. Larson (eds.), *Leadership: The Cutting Edge.* Carbondale: Southern Illinois University Press, pp. 189–207.

Howell, William G. and Terry M. Moe. 2020. *Presidents, Populism, and the Crisis of Democracy.* Chicago: University of Chicago Press.

Huang Zongxi. 1993. *Waiting for the Dawn: A Plan for the Prince*, trans. and ed. Wm. Theodore de Bary. New York: Columbia University Press.

Ibarra, Herminia, Claudius A. Hildebrand, and Sabine Vinck. 2023. "The Leadership Odyssey." *Harvard Business Review* 101:3 (May-June), pp. 102–110.

Ignatius, Adi. 2011. "The HBR Interview: Technology, Tradition, and the Mouse." Interview with Bob Iger. *Harvard Business Review* 89:7/8 (July–August), pp. 112–117.

2022. "HBS Professor Linda Hill Says Leaders Must Engage with Emotions as Never Before." Interview with Linda Hill. *Harvard Business Review* (March 11). https://hbr.org/2022/03/hbs-professor-linda-hill-says-leaders-must-engage-with-emotions-as-never-before.

Ignatius of Loyola, Saint. 1991. *The Spiritual Exercises and Selected Works*, ed. George E. Ganss. New York: Paulist Press.

Ihimaera, Witi. 1987. *The Whale Rider*. Auckland: Heinemann.

Jecker, Nancy S. 2021. "Nothing to Be Ashamed of: Sex Robots for Older Adults with Disabilities." *Journal of Medical Ethics* 47:1 (January), pp. 26–32.

Johnson, Mary. 2012. *An Unquenchable Thirst: A Memoir*. New York: Spiegel & Grau.

Jung, Carl G. 1963. *Memories, Dreams, Reflections*, ed. Aniela Jaffé, trans. Richard and Clara Winston. New York: Vintage.

Kanogo, Tabitha. 2020. *Wangari Maathai*. Ohio Short Histories of Africa. Athens: Ohio University Press.

Kant, Immanuel. 1991. "Idea for a General History with a Cosmopolitan Purpose." In *Political Writings*, trans. H. B. Nisbet, ed. Hans Reiss, 2nd enlarged ed. Cambridge: Cambridge University Press, pp. 41–53.

Kidder, Rushworth. 2005. *Moral Courage*. New York: William Morrow.

Kimmerer, Robin Wall. 2002. "Weaving Traditional Ecological Knowledge into Biological Education: A Call to Action." *Bioscence* 52:5 (May), pp. 432–438.

King, Martin Luther, Jr. 1986. *A Testament of Hope: The Essential Writings and Speeches of Martin Luther King, Jr.*, ed. James Melvin Washington. New York: HarperCollins.

Kirsch, Noah. 2023. "How Prince Harry's $5 Billion Startup Went South." *Yahoo News* (August 5). https://news.yahoo.com/prince-harry-5-billion-startup-044345869.html.

Koestler, Arthur. 2019 [1941]. *Darkness at Noon*. New York: Scribner.

Kolbert, Elizabeth. 2014. *The Sixth Extinction: An Unnatural History*. New York: Henry Holt.

Kott, Jan. 1966. "Hamlet of the Mid-Century." In *Shakespeare Our Contemporary*, trans. Boleslaw Taborski. Garden City: Doubleday, pp. 57–73.

Kotz, Nick. 2005. *Judgment Days: Lyndon Baines Johnson, Martin Luther King Jr., and the Laws That Changed America*. New York: Houghton Mifflin.

Kowitt, Beth and Colleen Leahey. 2013. "Do you speak Lululemon?" CNN/Money (August 29). http://management.fortune.cnn.com/2013/08/29/lululemon-glossary/?iid=EL.

Kushner, Tony. 2012. *Lincoln: The Screenplay*. New York: Theatre Communications Group.

Ladkin, Donna. 2015. *Mastering the Ethical Dimension of Organizations*. Cheltenham: Edward Elgar.

Laozi. 2005. *Daode Jing*, trans. Tim Chilcott. https://dokumen.tips/documents/daode-jing-tao-te-ching-tim-chilcott-literary-tzu-tao-te-ching-introduction.html.

Lee, Robert E., Jr. 2019. *Recollections and Letters of General Robert E. Lee*. New York: Nova Science Publishers.

Lévi-Strauss, Claude. 1961 [1955]. *Tristes Tropiques*, trans. John Russell. New York: Criterion Books.

Levi, Primo. 1996. *Survival in Auschwitz*. New York: Touchstone.

Liker, Jeffrey K. 2004. *The Toyota Way: 14 Management Principles from the World's Greatest Manufacturer*. New York: McGraw-Hill.

Lincoln, Abraham. 1953. *Collected Works of Abraham* Lincoln, ed. Roy P. Basler. 9 vols. New Brunswick, NJ: Rutgers University Press.

Lindholm, Charles. 1990. *Charisma*. London: Blackwell.

  2021. "The Anthropology of Charisma." *Routledge International Handbook of Charisma*. New York: Routledge, ed. José Pedro Zúquete, pp. 39–50.

Louv, Richard. 2008. *Last Child in the Woods: Saving Our Children from Nature-Deficit Disorder*. Chapel Hill: Algonquin Books.

Ma, Li and Anne S. Tsui. 2015. "Traditional Chinese Philosophies and Contemporary Leadership." *The Leadership Quarterly* 26(1) (February), pp. 13–24.

Maathai, Wangari. 2004. Nobel Lecture. Oslo (November 10). www.nobelprize.org/prizes/peace/2004/maathai/lecture/

Machiavelli, Niccolò. 1985. *The Prince*, trans. and ed. Harvey C. Mansfield, Jr. Chicago: University of Chicago Press.

Malcolm, X. 1965. *Malcom X Speaks: Selected Speeches and Statements*, ed. George Breitman. New York: Grove Weidenfeld.

Mandela, Nelson. 1995. *Long Walk to Freedom*. Boston: Little, Brown.

Marean, Curtis W. 2015. "An Evolutionary Anthropological Perspective on Modern Human Origins." *Annual Review of Anthropology* 44, pp. 533–556.

Marlow, Louise, ed. 2023. *Medieval Muslim Mirrors for Princes: An Anthology of Arabic, Persian and Turkish Political Advice*. Cambridge: Cambridge University Press.

Marquardt, Michael. 2005. *Leading with Questions: How Leaders Find the Right Solutions by Knowing What to Ask*. San Francisco: Jossey-Bass.

Martin, James. 2000. *In Good Company: The Fast Track from the Corporate World to Poverty, Chastity and Obedience*. Lanham, MD: Rowman & Littlefield.

Maybury-Lewis, David. 1992. *Millennium: Tribal Wisdom and the Modern World*. New York: Viking.

Mayer, John D., Peter Salovey, and David R. Caruso. 2004. "Emotional Intelligence: Theory, Findings, and Implications." *Psychological Inquiry* 15:3, pp. 197–215.

McManus, Robert M. and Gamaliel Perruci. 2020. *Understanding Leadership: An Arts and Humanities Perspective*, 2nd ed. New York: Routledge.

Menkiti, Ifeanyi. 1984. "Person and Community in African Traditional Thought." In Richard A. Wright, ed., *African Philosophy: An Introduction*, 3rd ed. Lanham, MD: University Press of America, pp. 171–181.

Minsky, Laurence and David Aaron. 2021. "Are You Doing the SWOT Analysis Backwards?" *Harvard Business Review* (February 23). Reprint H067M6. https://hbr.org/2021/02/are-you-doing-the-swot-analysis-backwards.

National Park Service. n.d. " 'If Virginia Stands by the Old Union' – Robert E. Lee Resigns from the U.S. Army." Web page. www.nps.gov/rich/learn/historyculture/-if-virginia-stands-by-the-old-union-robert-e-lee-resigns-from-the-u-s-army.htm.

Neely, Tucker. 2009. "A Catalyst for Change, by Way of Kenya: Wangari Maathai's Vision for Africa Is 'Taking Root.' " *Washington Post* (April 18), p. C3.

Nightingale, Florence. 2002–2014. *The Collected Works of Florence Nightingale*, ed. Lynn McDonald, 16 vols. Waterloo: Wilfrid Laurier University Press.

Oates, Stephen B. Oates. 1977. *With Malice Toward None: The Life of Abraham Lincoln*. New York: Harper & Row.

Okolo, Mary Stella Chika. 2007. *African Literature as Political Philosophy*. Dakar, Senegal: Codesria Books and London: Zed Books.

Orwell, George. 2021. *1984 and Animal Farm*. London: Collins Classics.

Page, Larry. 2015. "G is for Google." Letter to Google employees. August 10. https://blog.google/alphabet/google-alphabet/

Parker, Lee D. and Philip A. Ritson. 2005. "Re-visiting Fayol: Anticipating Contemporary Management." *British Journal of Management* 16:3 (September), pp. 175–194.

Payments Journal. 2019. "How Many Bank Accounts Do Consumers Have?" (July 2). www.paymentsjournal.com/how-many-bank-accounts-do-con sumers-have/

Pelling, Christopher. 2002. *Plutarch and History: Eighteen Studies*. Swansea: Classical Press of Wales.

Perlez, Jane. 1989. "Plan for Sun-Hogging Tower Angers Kenyans." *New York Times* (November 26). www.nytimes.com/1989/11/26/world/plan-for-sun-hogging-tower-angers-kenyans.html.

Peterson, Jillian and James Densley. 2021. *The Violence Project: How to Stop a Mass Shooting Epidemic*. New York: Abrams Press.

Pieterse, Cosmo and Dennis Duerden, eds. 1972. *African Writers Talking: A Collection of Radio Interviews*. New York: Africana.

Pitkin, Hanna Fenichel. 1984. *Fortune Is a Woman: Gender and Politics in the Thought of Niccolò Machiavelli*. Berkeley: University of California Press.

Plato. 1991. *The Republic*, trans. and ed. Allan Bloom, 2nd ed. New York: Basic Books.

1995. *Statesman*, trans. Robin Waterfield, eds. Julia Annas and Robin Waterfield. Cambridge: Cambridge University Press.

Porter, Catherine, Constant Méheut, Matt Apuzzo, and Selam Gebrekidan. 2022. "The Ransom: The Root of Haiti's Misery: Reparations to Enslavers." *New York Times* (May 20). www.nytimes.com/2022/05/20/world/americas/haiti-history-colonized-france.html.

Porter, Michael E. 1979. "How Competitive Forces Shape Strategy." *Harvard Business Review* 57:2 (March-April), pp. 137–145.

Price, Terry L. 2008. *Leadership Ethics: An Introduction*. New York: Cambridge University Press.

Protocol of the Wannsee Conference, January 20, 1942. 2020. Berlin: House of the Wannsee Conference. www.ghwk.de/en/conference/protocol-and-documents.

Pryor, Mildred Golden, Donna Anderson, Leslie A. Toombs, and John H. Humphreys. 2007. "Strategic Implementation as a Core Competency." *Journal of Management Research* 7:1 (April), p. 3.

Putnam, Robert D. 2000. *Bowling Alone: The Collapse and Revival of American Community*. New York: Simon & Schuster.

Ramaswamy, Tumkur N., ed. 2007. *Essentials of Indian Statecraft: Kautilya's Arthasastra for Contemporary Readers*. New Delhi: South Asia Books.

Ramose, Mogobe B. 1999. *African Philosophy through Ubuntu*. Harare, Zimbabwe: Mond Books.

Reave, Laura. 2005. "Spiritual Values and Practices Related to Leadership Effectiveness." *Leadership Quarterly* 16:5 (October), pp. 655–688.

Reingold, Jennifer. 2014. "How to Fail in Business While Really, Really Trying," *Fortune* (March 20).

Reese, George H., ed. 1965. *Proceedings of the Virginia State Convention of 1861: February 13-May 1, 1861*, 4 vols. Richmond: Virginia State Library. https://fortune.com/2014/03/20/how-to-fail-in-business-while-really-really-trying/.

Richter, Felix. 2021. "Covid-19 Vaccines: From Zero to 11.2 Billion in a Year." *Statista* (Dec. 17). www.statista.com/chart/26420/global-covid-19-vaccine-production/.

Riggio, Ronald. 2006. "Charisma." *Encyclopedia of Leadership*. Eds. James MacGregor Burns, G. R. Goethals, and Georgia J. Sorenson. Sage Reference, 2004.

2013. *Introduction to Industrial/Organizational Psychology*, 6th ed. New York: Pearson.

Riggio, Ronald E. and Jay A. Conger. 2008. *The Practice of Leadership: Developing the Next Generation of Leaders*. San Francisco: Jossey-Bass.

Ross, Lee. 1977. "The Intuitive Psychologist and His Shortcomings: Distortions in the Attribution Process." In Leonard Berkowitz, ed., *Advances in Experimental Social Psychology*, Vol. 10. New York: Academic Press, pp. 173–220.

Russell, Daniel C. 2014. "Phronesis and the Virtues (*NE* vi 12–13)." *The Cambridge Companion to Aristotle's Nicomachean Ethics*, ed. Ronald Polansky. New York: Cambridge University Press.

Schein, Edgar. 2009. *The Corporate Culture Survival Guide*, rev. ed. San Francisco: Jossey-Bass.

2010. *Organizational Culture and Leadership*, 4th ed. San Francisco: Jossey-Bass.

Scott, James C. 2017. *Against the Grain: A Deep History of the Earliest States*. New Haven: Yale University Press.

Sears, Priscilla. 1991. "Wangari Maathai: 'You Strike the Woman. . . .' " *In Context*, #28 (Spring), pp. 55–57. www.context.org/iclib/ic28/sears.

Seidman, Dov. 2007. *How: Why How We Do Anything Means Everything*, expanded ed. Hoboken, NJ: John Wiley & Sons.

Shakespeare, William. 1969. *The Complete Works*, gen. ed. Alfred Harbage. The Pelican Text revised. New York: Viking Press.

Simpson, William Kelly, ed. 2003. *The Literature of Ancient Egypt: An Anthology of Stories, Instructions, Stelae, Autobiographies, and Poetry.* New Haven: Yale University Press.

Sinek, Simon. 2009. *Start with Why: How Great Leaders Inspire Everyone to Take Action.* New York: Portfolio.

Sissons, Jeffrey. 2005. *First Peoples: Indigenous Cultures and Their Futures.* London: Reaktion Books, 2005.

Skirbekk, Vegard. 2022. *Decline and Prosper: Changing Global Birth Rates and the Advantages of Fewer Children.* London: Palgrave Macmillan.

Sloan, Alfred. 1990 [1963]. *My Years at General Motors.* Eds. John McDonald and Catharine Stevens. New York: Currency Doubleday.

Smith, Adam. 1759. *The Theory of Moral Sentiments*, 2nd ed. London: A. Millar.

Smith, Adam. 1776. *An Inquiry into the Nature and Causes of the Wealth of Nations.* Ed. C. J. Bullock. New York :P. F. Collier.

Spada, Giorgio and Gaia Galassi. 2017. "Extent and Dynamic Evolution of the Lost Land Aquaterra since the Last Glacial Maximum." *Comptes Rendus Geoscience* 349:4 (July–August), pp. 151–158.

Stephens, Alexander H. 2008. "Cornerstone Speech," In *The Civil War and Reconstruction: A Documentary Reader*, ed. Stanley Harrold. Malden, MA: Blackwell, pp. 59–63.

Stewart-Williams, Steve. 2018. *The Ape that Understood the Universe: How the Mind and Culture Evolve.* New York: Cambridge University Press.

St. George, Zach. 2022. "Can Planting a Trillion New Trees Save the World?" *New York Times Magazine* (July 13). www.nytimes.com/2022/07/13/maga zine/planting-trees-climate-change.html

Stogdill, Ralph M. 1974. *Handbook of Leadership: A Survey of the Literature.* New York: Free Press.

Stone, Isidor F. 1988. *The Trial of Socrates.* Boston: Little, Brown.

Stowe, Harriet Beecher. 1873. *Woman in Sacred History.* New York: J. B. Ford.

Stumpf, John G. 2015. *The Vision & Values of Wells Fargo.* Wells Fargo.

Suleyman, Mustafa and Michael Bhaskar. 2023. *The Coming Wave: Technology, Power, and the Twenty-first Century's Greatest Dilemma.* New York: Crown.

Sullivan, Vickie, ed. 2000. *The Comedy and Tragedy of Machiavelli: Essays on the Literary Works.* New Haven: Yale University Press.

Summitt, Pat and Sally Jenkins. 1998a. *Raise the Roof.* New York: Broadway Books.

1998b. *Reach for the Summitt: The Definite Dozen System for Succeeding at Whatever You Do.* New York: Broadway Books.

2013. *Sum It Up*. New York: Three Rivers Press.

Taylor, Christopher C. W. 1998. *Socrates: A Very Short Introduction*. New York: Oxford University Press.

Taylor, Frederick. 1998 [1911]. *Principles of Scientific Management*. Mineola: Dover.

Teresa, Mother. 2007. *Come Be My Light: The Private Writings of the "Saint of Calcutta,"* ed. Brian Kolodiejchuk. New York: Doubleday.

Terkel, Studs. 1974. *Working: People Talk About What They Do All Day and How They Feel About What They Do*. New York: Ballantine.

Turkle, Sherry. 2012. *Alone Together: Why We Expect More from Technology and Less from Each Other*. New York: Basic Books.

van Vugt, Mark and Richard Ronay. 2014. "The Evolutionary Psychology of Leadership: Theory, Review, and Roadmap." *Organizational Psychology Review* 4:1 (January), pp. 74–95,

Venkatesh, Sudhir. 2008. *Gang Leader for a Day*. New York: Penguin.

Vidal, John. 2011. "Wangari Maathai Obituary." *The Guardian* (September 26). www.theguardian.com/world/2011/sep/26/wangari-maathai.

Vlastos, Gregor. 1991. *Socrates: Ironist and Moral Philosopher*. Ithaca: Cornell University Press.

Wachtel, Eleanor. 1994. "Chinua Achebe on redefining Nigeria with his writing," CBC radio interview. www.cbc.ca/radio/writersandcompany/chinua-achebe-on-redefining-nigeria-with-his-writing-1.3689009.

Walzer, Michael. 2012. *In God's Shadow: Politics in the Hebrew Bible*. New Haven: Yale University Press.

Weaver, David R. 1997. "Leadership, Locke, and the Federalist." *American Journal of Political Science* 41:2 (April), pp. 420–446.

Weber, Max 1978. *Economy and Society: An Outline of Interpretive Sociology*, eds. Guenther Roth and Claus Wittich. 2 vols. Berkeley: University of California Press.

Welch, Jack and John A. Byrne. 2001. *Jack: Straight from the Gut*. New York: Warner Books.

Whitman, Walt. 2001. *Leaves of Grass: The "Death-Bed" Edition*. New York: Modern Library.

Williams, Linda L. 1996. "Will to Power in Nietzsche's Published Works and the *Nachlass*." *Journal of the History of Ideas* 57:3 (July), pp. 447–463. www.jstor.org/stable/3653949.

Wilson, Woodrow. 1900. *Congressional Government: A Study in American Politics*, 15th ed. Boston: Houghton Mifflin.

Wollstonecraft, Mary. 1992. *A Vindication of the Rights of Woman*, ed. Miriam Brody. New York: Penguin Books.

Woodruff, Paul. 1998. "Socratic Education." In *Philosophers on Education: New Historical Perspectives*, ed. Amélie Oksenberg Rorty. New York: Routledge, pp. 13–29.

Wren, J. Thomas, ed. 1995. *The Leader's Companion: Insights on Leadership Through the Ages*. New York: Free Press.

Yarber, Aara'L. 2023. "Humans Have Used Enough Groundwater to Shift Earth's Tilt." *Washington Post* (June 27). www.washingtonpost.com/science/2023/06/27/groundwater-use-planet-earth-tilt/.

Yasir, Sameer. 2020. "Gandhi's Killer Evokes Admiration as Never Before." *New York Times* (February 4). www.nytimes.com/2020/02/04/world/asia/india-gandhi-nathuram-godse.html

Yukl, Gary. 2010. *Leadership in Organizations*, 7th ed. Upper Saddle River: Prentice Hall.

Acknowledgments

For Ida Rosenblatt Wolle
1872–1942

Ronald E. Riggio
Claremont McKenna College

Ronald E. Riggio, PhD is the Henry R. Kravis Professor of Leadership and Organisational Psychology and former Director of the Kravis Leadership Institute at Claremont McKenna College. Dr. Riggio is a psychologist and leadership scholar with over a dozen authored or edited books and more than 150 articles/book chapters. He has worked as a consultant, and serves on multiple editorial boards.

Susan E. Murphy
University of Edinburgh

Susan E. Murphy is Chair in Leadership Development at the University of Edinburgh Business School. She has published numerous articles and book chapters on leadership, leadership development, and mentoring. Susan was formerly Director of the School of Strategic Leadership Studies at James Madison University and Professor of Leadership Studies. Prior to that, she served as faculty and associate director of the Henry R. Kravis Leadership Institute at Claremont McKenna College. She also serves on the editorial board of *The Leadership Quarterly*.

Georgia Sorenson
University of Cambridge

The late Georgia Sorenson, PhD, was the James MacGregor Burns Leadership Scholar at the Moller Institute and Moller By-Fellow of Churchill College at Cambridge University. Before coming to Cambridge, she founded the James MacGregor Burns Academy of Leadership at the University of Maryland, where she was Distinguished Research Professor. An architect of the leadership studies field, Dr. Sorenson has authored numerous books and refereed journal articles.

About the Series

Cambridge Elements in Leadership is multi- and inter-disciplinary, and will have broad appeal for leadership courses in Schools of Business, Education, Engineering, Public Policy, and in the Social Sciences and Humanities

Cambridge Elements $\equiv$

Leadership

Elements in the Series

A full series listing is available at: www.cambridge.org/CELE